Alfred Hitchcock

Alfred Hitchcock

THE MAN WHO KNEW TOO MUCH

MICHAEL WOOD

ICONS SERIES

New Harvest
Houghton Mifflin Harcourt
BOSTON • NEW YORK
2015

This edition published by special arrangement with Amazon Publishing

For information about permission to reproduce selections from this book, go to www.apub.com.

www.hmhco.com

Library of Congress Cataloging-in-Publication Data
Wood, Michael, date.
Alfred Hitchcock : the man who knew too much / Michael Wood.
pages   cm. — (Icons series)
ISBN 978-0-544-45622-8 (hardback)
1. Hitchcock, Alfred, 1899–1980. 2. Motion picture producers
and directors — Great Britain — Biography. I. Title.
PN1998.3.H58W64 2015
791.4302'33092 — dc23
[B]
2014039691

Printed in the United States of America
DOC 10 9 8 7 6 5 4 3 2 1

And really he was too much like one of us not to be dangerous.
—Joseph Conrad, *Lord Jim*

Contents

Alfred Hitchcock

First Steps

A Touch of Class

ALFRED HITCHCOCK WAS born a few years after the advent of cinema and just before the twentieth century began, on August 13, 1899. He grew up in East London, the child of a hardworking, serious Catholic family. His father owned and ran a greengrocer's shop and the family lived above it; the father, with his brothers, also had an interest in a wholesale fruit and vegetable business. The Hitchcocks were not rich, not poor; they were rising in the world, but there wasn't far for them to rise. Their class had dignity and self-respect, but it didn't have the privileges of the upper orders and the haute bourgeoisie, and it didn't have the solidarity and burgeoning energy of the newly self-conscious working classes (the British Labour Party would be founded in 1900). Margaret Thatcher, born a quarter century later and decidedly *not* a member of the Labour Party, belonged to much the same class as the Hitchcocks and could be said never to have left it in her manners, dress, and assumptions — only her (diligently acquired) accent and pitch of voice suggested a personality accustomed to command. I don't want to claim that class, even in England, determines everything or even most things, but it's worth noting that members of the Hitchcock/Thatcher category are likely to have certain perspectives in common: an eye for the market, a distrust of the state, a healthy disapproval of people who are too

posh and people who are too disreputable, and a firm conviction that if you want something done you should do it yourself.

Hitchcock's father has entered legend less as an authoritar-
ian than as a man who liked authority. He is supposed to have
sent his son to the police station with a note saying he had mis-
behaved and asking the constable in charge to please lock the
small offender up for a time. Hitchcock claimed he always remembered "the clang of the door . . . the sound and the solidity
of that closing cell door and the bolt." He would have been four
years old at the time, or perhaps eleven, or perhaps . . . His age
changed with different tellings of the story. Its general outline
was confirmed by Hitchcock's sister, but of course she may have
been only preserving a family legend. I don't see why it couldn't
be true, but even if it is, its symbolic import far outweighs any
documentary effect. This is a myth of origin for a distrust of authority, and in Hitchcock's films this distrust takes a very particular form: the inability to believe that policemen, or any other
figures of institutional command, know how to do anything except take orders or collude with father figures (or fathers). This
means that they will, in one way or another and almost infalli-
bly, get things wrong. They are not to blame if they can't think
for themselves, or if reality is too difficult or elusive for them;
but they are not to be relied on either.

Patrick McGilligan, author of the most substantial Hitchcock biography, counters this story with the report that "Alfred
was so well behaved as a boy, his father dubbed him 'my little
lamb without a spot.'" I don't find the two stories completely
incompatible. In my English childhood, the question "Have
you been good?" meant "Have you not caused anybody any
trouble?" Indeed, "good" often meant entirely passive or even
fast asleep, incapable of mischief for the moment. And we could
read Hitchcock's lifelong worry about policemen in this simpler way too. He was afraid, not of being locked up as an innocent man, but of being found out as a mild offender — he was

his own policeman and scarcely ever drove a car for fear of driving badly. His wife, Alma, said that once after having "swerved slightly across a white line in England" and being pulled over and warned by the police, he spent days wondering whether he was going to be summoned to appear in court.

Another childhood scene is less dramatic but more haunting, I find, and leads us into other regions of Hitchcock's movies. John Russell Taylor, Hitchcock's first biographer — who presumably had the story directly from Hitchcock — recounts that the child woke up "around eight o'clock one Sunday evening to find that his parents were out and there was only the maid watching over him in his room." This fact "made an unaccountably profound impression on him ... [and] produced such a feeling of desolation and abandonment that he still remembered it when he got married." Young Alfred would not be the first or last child to feel that a babysitter was no substitute for a parent, nor was he the first or last member of the middle class to have restricted ideas about the capacities of maids. What's remarkable here, I think, and would be remarkable in any similar case, is the implied or discovered fear. Not just: *My parents have abandoned me,* but: *I always knew they would.* Hitchcock's films are full of premonitory fears of this kind, often all the more powerful because they turn out to be unfounded. If the event doesn't justify them, as it certainly did not in Hitchcock's personal case, what does justify them, and why don't they go away?

These fears, of abandonment and incarceration and much else, are not unusual and do not indicate a troubled childhood. But they do suggest a slightly beleaguered sense of existence, and I am persuaded by Taylor's picture of a plump, secretive, watchful child, convinced that if he stepped out of line in any way, if he revealed anything of what he thought and felt, betrayed his emotions to anyone else, *they* (the harsh, rationalistic, disapproving "they" of Edward Lear's nonsense poems) would somehow come and get him.

As a child Alfred attended several Catholic schools in East London before settling in at St. Ignatius College in Stamford Hill for his secondary education. This was a Jesuit school, and therefore, to a large extent, it shared the curriculum of other schools of the same denomination at home and abroad: Clongowes Wood College in Dublin, for example, where James Joyce was a pupil from 1888 to 1891, and Colegio del Salvador in Saragossa, where Luis Buñuel, born in 1900, was a pupil from 1908 to 1915. The school was strict but wide-ranging in the topics taught, and even hellfire, part of the required curriculum, could burn differently in different places. It was milder at St. Ignatius than at Clongowes Wood. Still, many critics have made a big deal out of Hitchcock's Jesuit instruction, and it does seem that everything that separates him from Joyce and Buñuel plays itself out against a ground of shared fidelity to old fears and orthodoxies. Fears can't be trivial, these artists suggest, whatever other people think, and orthodoxies can't be abandoned or contradicted until you have given them your full attention.

Hitchcock seems to have been fairly lonely in school, although he did make one or two friends he stayed in touch with for the rest of his life. He was shy and not keen on mixing with the other pupils, but he did well academically and was confident about his abilities. He was among many boys whose families were better off than his was, and who themselves thought they were likely to be ruling the world one day soon. He knew how clever he was, but also knew he was headed for different pursuits. He knew this not because he had decided where he was going but because he knew the direction would depend on him. He believed in luck, and over his film career became more and more preoccupied with chance and its strange apparitions. But he thought a person could do a lot to make luck come to him rather than pass him by.

Hitchcock put this belief into practice as soon as he left

school. He was fourteen years old. He took courses in an array of scientific subjects at the London County Council School of Engineering and Navigation and later attended art classes at Goldsmiths College. His interests in design and construction were becoming clear. He found a job where, after a spell of rather miscellaneous beginner's tasks, he entered the sales department. As McGilligan says, if Hitchcock had been something of an oddity at St. Ignatius College, the reverse was true at W. T. Henley's Telegraph Works, where "he was decidedly well known and well liked." His father died in 1914, when Alfred was fifteen years old, a month or so after he started work; a severe shock but only one of many, alas, in a country that had been at war since July of the same year. There had never been any plan for Alfred to take over the family business, so he was free to continue the career he had found.

Henley's was a company that manufactured electric cables and motor tires, and apart from the pleasures of devising advertising gimmicks and campaigns, which never left him — his television career was in many ways a resumption of this old trade — Hitchcock was able to write stories for the firm's magazine, the *Henley Telegraph*. In hindsight, they seem remarkably Hitchcockian, especially the one called "Fedora," which tells us that "every person has a plot and every plot is the same," before going on to demonstrate that a plot is not what happens to people but what we think might happen to them. His heroine is "small, simple, unassuming, and noiseless," but she catches everyone's attention. The narrator thinks perhaps she will become a politician or an actress. Or will she marry the mayor of some large city? "It is all conjecture on my part," Hitchcock writes. "I am no prophet; neither is she."

Every plot is the same perhaps because every plot is a fiction; it closes the otherwise unclosable account, turns the future into the perfected past.

Two-Part Inventions

Hitchcock spent hours at the theater and the movies, roamed all over London, and knew every bus and tram route by heart. In later years, in California, the number 24 would crop up, and he would murmur, as if he were dipping a madeleine into his gin, "Ah, yes, Hampstead Heath to Victoria" — then as now the route of the 24 bus. He had become, or was becoming, what he would always remain: a sort of inventor. He put things together and made new things of the combination. He found new ways of looking at things. He found new things to look at. If Orson Welles said the movies were the biggest electric train set a boy ever had, Hitchcock might have said they were a magical, unscientific laboratory, a place for the confection of gadgets and toys that played with our minds as much as our minds played with them.

He was often accused of excessive trickery in his films, especially early in his career, and it is true that he loved tricks of all kinds. But the tricks were miniature ways of looking at the world, not always successfully communicated but always in pursuit of something more than an effect; as Hitchcock got older and his films unfolded their inventions, nothing looked like mere trickery anymore, and the miniature had become very large. And yet. Try filming the centerpiece of *North by Northwest:* an attempt to kill someone by bullets fired from a crop-dusting plane in an empty midwestern landscape. It's a lot harder than actually killing someone by the same method, and why would you want to do that anyway? Only an inventor would think of it.

When Famous Players-Lasky, an American film company, announced its intention of opening a studio in Islington, London, Hitchcock prepared himself. He had heard that the studio was interested in adapting Marie Corelli's *The Sorrows of Satan,* so he wrote a treatment and showed it to the executives. They weren't that interested in the treatment (and never made the film), but they saw his promise and hired him. For quite a while he composed title cards — not a minor job in the world of silent films. Between 1920 and 1922 he worked on seven films in this role, followed by five films on which he was title designer and art director. He got his first chance at directing with *Number 13,* which remained unfinished, and continued to work as an assistant director, art director, and writer on six more films.

When Famous Players closed its London operation in 1922, Hitchcock went to work for Michael Balcon, his first fan and patron, who, with Victor Saville and Jack Freedman, had formed Gainsborough Pictures and taken over the Islington studio. Hitchcock made five films for Balcon in the 1920s and returned to work with him again for a series of great films in the 1930s.

Hitchcock worked a lot with the director Graham Cutts, taking on more responsibilities with each film. His second chance to direct on his own came with a joint English-German production called *The Pleasure Garden* (1925). This was a steamy and rather predictable story of two chorus girls in London, one a fortune hunter, the other a nice girl who marries a man she doesn't yet know is a philanderer. His adulterous affairs continue in the tropics while she remains at home, and he murders his mistress when his wife comes to visit. He drunkenly tries to kill his wife too but is shot just in time, and she survives to marry the other guy, the one who has loved her all along.

The death of the erring husband is the high point of the film and for a very Hitchcockian reason. When he is shot he comes to his senses, no longer drunk at all; he mildly says, "Oh, hello, Doctor," to the man who has interrupted his fury and dies. The German producer at the studio where Hitchcock shot this scene was outraged and shouted, "It's impossible. You can't show a scene like this. It's incredible and too brutal." The outrage no doubt only confirmed Hitchcock's sense of the interest of what he was doing, and he kept the scene. Later in life he was surprised to learn how difficult and time consuming it can be to kill a person, and the one good moment in *Torn Curtain* (1966) has Paul Newman laboriously stuffing a man into a stove. There is a sense, though, in which a casual, almost negligent registering of one's last moment is scarier — not brutal or incredible as the German producer thought, but too natural for art, as if the erratic truth of death's timing were more than we could bear in a story. Hitchcock plainly thought a lot about this matter, since he repeated the effect at the beginning of the first *Man Who Knew Too Much* (1934) and later went on record as believing the death of any character in a film should never be taken lightly. It is a brilliant move, of course, to take death seriously by having the character take it far too lightly.

Hitchcock had met Alma Reville at work. She had started at Famous Players-Lasky four years before he did, in charge of continuity on several films, including D. W. Griffith's *Hearts of the World,* and serving as assistant director on several more. She was in this sense Hitchcock's senior, although she was chronologically a few hours his junior; she was born on August 14, 1899. Hitchcock was extremely conscious of this edge, or said he was, and claimed that he couldn't ask her to marry him until he had risen to the role of at least assistant director. This he did (rise and propose) in 1925, and they were married in Brompton Oratory on December 2, 1926.

Alma was born in Nottingham. Her family, fairly well-to-do, moved to London soon after her birth. It is well known that from the start Hitchcock made few, if any, decisions without consulting her, and up through 1950 she received formal credits on many of his films. Her last credit was for the adaptation of *Stage Fright.* There is every reason to believe that her role in thinking about, setting up, and making judgments about films in progress remained as large as it ever was, credit or no credit, and the story told about her intervention in *Psycho* (1960) may be taken to stand for many similar moments that were not known beyond the Hitchcock household creative consultancy. A large number of people, including Hitchcock himself, had closely scrutinized the dailies of the sequence where Janet Leigh's character, Marion Crane, is killed in the shower. Everything seemed fine. When Leigh played dead, she looked dead. No, Alma said, there is one shot in which she blinks — you have to fix it. She was right: The brief, all but invisible blink was there.

When we think of Hitchcock's films we need always to think of the help he got, the many remarkable writers, cameramen, actors, designers, musicians, and others who worked with him. But we have to think of Alma as part of Hitchcock himself, I believe, in the sense of presiding over his work as an artistic intelligence. He would have been something without her, no doubt, but he would not have been the director we know as Hitchcock.

Alma was a private person, intensely loyal to her husband, protective of him and patient with him. He guarded her privacy with some care, although he liked to fence it with jokes about her that often seemed blunt or even unkind. Alma no doubt read them differently. Or she liked their bluntness and knew they were not unkind. She can't have lived with Hitchcock for fifty-four years without knowing he liked to pretend to be "Hitchcock." We know very little about what she thought, but we do know how firm and intelligent she was, and how attentive to Hitchcock and the world; and we know, from the films *Hitchcock* and *The Girl* (both 2012), that she is not Helen Mirren or Imelda Staunton. Both actresses play their parts well and make real contributions to these biopics about the director. It's just that the director isn't Hitchcock and Alma isn't Alma. He's not Hitchcock because he is a ready-made cliché of the artist in crisis into which Hitchcock's name has been slotted. And she is not Alma because the character isn't elusive enough, too snippy in Mirren's performance and too submissive in Staunton's. Whoever Alma was, she was more complicated, more secret than this. We could take this as a working definition of her, perhaps: If you could show her in a movie, or even in a biography, you would have missed her, missed the wit that ensured her escape from you. Pat Hitchcock's memoir of her mother, full of affection and good memories (and recipes), confirms this view rather than refutes it. Alma's privacy is still safe. Fortunately, Hitchcock himself is not so adept at getting away.

On their return from their honeymoon in 1927, the Hitchcocks took an apartment on Cromwell Road in London and later bought a house in the country, at Shamley Green in Surrey. In America they repeated this pattern: main residence in the Bel Air neighborhood in Los Angeles, country place near Santa Cruz, California. Alma really liked California. Hitchcock said, "It was love at first smell." They were never poor and became rather affluent. They lived well, ate well, and drank well, and traveled quite a bit. But they didn't behave like rich people and they didn't think they were rich, even when they were. John Russell Taylor describes how he met their daughter as she was leaving her parents' house "in a state of some irritation":

> [W]hen she arrived to visit the parents she had found them deep in a painful discussion about whether, if he were to go first (at this time they were both 79), she could afford to go on living in Bel Air. "I found myself screaming 'For heaven's sake, everyone knows you are one of the richest men in Hollywood, still working, still getting masses of residuals. If you never earned another penny, you couldn't spend everything you have if you lived to be two hundred. Why do you torture yourselves like this?' All he said was 'You never know. One has to consider all possibilities.'"

This maxim, while annoying in life and not really connected to simple reason — if the Hitchcocks wanted to worry they would, like anyone else, find something to worry about — could serve as a theory of Hitchcock's films. One has to consider all the possibilities, especially when they are not practically possible.

Patricia, the Hitchcocks' only child, was born in 1928. On the basis of the films and the many legends about the director, we might think it was more than a little daunting to be Hitchcock's daughter, but Pat, as she prefers to be called, will have none of this. Even the often repeated story of her waking up to find her face painted with a scary mask brings amused memories to her rather than thoughts of old terrors. And when she addresses the question of her father's sadism, it is in the form of a joke about money, not uncharacteristic of the man himself. He did offer her a hundred dollars to ride on the Ferris wheel in *Strangers on a Train* (1951), but he didn't, as has been suggested, leave her there for hours. "The only sadistic part," Pat said, "was I never got the hundred dollars." What we learn from Pat — her book, her interviews, the photographs of her and her children with her parents — is that Hitchcock was a family man, and not just an imitation of one. This is no doubt one of the reasons why his preferred films often represent families in danger, and why his cameo appearance in *Torn Curtain* shows him holding a small child on his lap. He knows all the risks, from kidnapping to lapses of toilet training.

The Right Wrong Man

Hitchcock later told long stories about the making of his first films as director — *The Pleasure Garden* and *The Mountain Eagle* — involving travels in Europe, shortages of money, confiscated film stock, and expensive, late-arriving stars. François Truffaut said of one of these tales that it was "more exciting than the scenario," and Hitchcock implied that it might have been more exciting than the finished film. And then, in 1926, he released *The Lodger,* in which he became Hitchcock — as if a certain kind of thriller, a certain murky London atmosphere, a context of rising hysteria, and the threat of extraordinary violence lurking on the edge of ordinary lives, had just been waiting for him to step up and affix his name to it. It hadn't just been waiting, of course. The materials were there, but only Hitchcock could produce their amazing precipitate. This film had to be invented, and he invented himself as an artist at the same time.

The opening of *The Lodger* is abrupt, even startling. We see a terrified woman's face but we don't know what is terrifying her. Bright lights flash out the words "To-night 'Golden Curls.'" This seems to be an advertisement for a show but there is no theater or street to be seen, just the words, the lights. Now we see a body lying on the ground, a frightened witness talking to a policeman, a crowd gathering. A card tells us the Avenger has struck again — has struck for the seventh time. We are on the Embankment in London. We see everyone talking about the crime — reporting on the radio, gossiping on the street, putting the news out in print. We even see the papers being made. "Wet from the press" is what it says on one of the title cards. Soon we are told that the killer specializes in blondes ("To-night 'Golden Curls'") and has a preference for Tuesdays.

The story starts, and we see why the film is called *The Lodger.* Daisy is a fashion model who lives with her not very well-off parents. She has a regular boyfriend who is a police detective and pretty dull. They are talking about the serial killer, and the boyfriend says he also likes golden hair — his idea of a compliment to Daisy, of course, but the connection is distinctly disturbing. Then the gaslight dims. There's a knock at the door. A dark, handsome man stands there looking haunted, his face half covered in a way that press reports have associated with the Avenger. Everyone — Daisy, boyfriend, parents — is scared.

But all is well, or may be well. The gaslight went down because the meter needed feeding. The visitor has come about the announced room to rent, and the potential lodger is played by Ivor Novello, even if he does at the moment resemble Bela Lugosi as he appears in those Dracula films that have not yet been made.

Hitchcock said he thought no studio or audience in the 1920s would believe Novello could represent a killer, or would want him to. In fact Hitchcock creates an image of Novello that keeps us wondering not whether he is the killer but what possible narrative twist could make him into something else. The solution is satisfactory enough: The lodger is tracking the killer, who murdered his sister, which is why his movements have been the same as the killer's. The point is that innocence and guilt leave many of the same traces. The point is not that there is no difference between them but that there is no difference between the reconstructions of their trail. The lodger is arrested as chief suspect, escapes, then is spotted in a pub and chased by a gesticulating mob, to end up dangling by his handcuffs from a spiked railing. The police and the mob have found their suspicions justified because they were justified, but only by appearances. Crowds are important in Hitchcock's work because they are the basic believers in the wrong story, its true congregation, so to speak, and films in this mode can tell the right story only by telling, or seeming to tell, the wrong story first.

Finally the actual Avenger is arrested and the lodger gets together with Daisy, to the delight of her now no longer suspicious parents. It's worth pausing over the brilliant last few shots. As the couple moves into a concluding embrace, the "To-night 'Golden Curls'" sign flashes out behind them. They kiss and the sign flashes again. We see Daisy's face in contented close-up, the lodger's image almost vanishing upward, leaving only his chin and teeth in view. This insistence on Daisy's blissful look — she is not just untroubled, but she has also banished the very idea of trouble from the universe; she looks like a person imitating

happiness in a movie — provides the film's one genuinely frightening (as distinct from riddling or intriguing) moment. But
why? Perhaps we think that this happy end is too close to what
might have been its unhappy reverse — remember everyone's
suspicions and the raging mob. Hitchcock may also be remind-
ing us that the capture of one serial killer doesn't abolish serial
killing, except within a particular plotline. There are fanciers of
golden curls everywhere — in the theater, on the streets, and in
the home — and one man's innocence does not rid the world of
guilt.

We might add that in the novel that is Hitchcock's source —
it had been turned into a play before it became a film — the
lodger *is* guilty, a man with a religious mania he takes out on
women; he has already established an impressive record in
Leipzig and Liverpool. There are continuities, though. If in the
film we worry about what the signs of guilt can mean if they
don't mean guilt, in the novel the husband and wife who house
the lodger worry about what to do with their suspicions of their
tenant's activities. They can't go to the police, because they're
afraid of all entanglements with the law; and at the end of the
novel they are grimly awaiting (but not really expecting) some
kind of release. At one point the husband has these truly Hitchcockian thoughts: "the most awful thing about it all was that he
wasn't sure . . . If only he really knew! If only he could feel quite
sure! And then he would tell himself that, after all, he had very
little to go upon; only suspicion — suspicion, and a secret, horrible certainty that his suspicion was justified." A suspicion that
is also a certainty, a certainty that is only a suspicion: logically
untenable states of mind, but something like second nature to
characters in Hitchcock.

One of Hitchcock's inventions in *The Lodger* was a glass ceil-
ing through which the feet of the suspected serial killer could
be seen pacing the floor upstairs. The scene caused all kinds of
trouble among the Gainsborough executives — they thought it

was flashy and unreal, in abominable taste — and the release of the film was suspended for several months. Hitchcock later said he thought the sequence was too obvious and that it would have been enough to have a few lamps or furnishings shake from the upstairs movement, indicating the troubled nerves and suspicions of the family downstairs. Watching the scene now, we are not inclined to claim it is subtle, but it is magical: an incontrovertible, perfectly placed picture of a fear that turns out to be perfectly misplaced.

2

Between the Wars

Something Very British

FOR A NAME and a body of work to last, to grow and change, it is not enough to invent them. One has to invent them again and again. Hitchcock did this, but not immediately. He made two more films for Gainsborough (*Downhill* and *Easy Virtue*, both 1927), then moved to British International Pictures, for whom he made a run of eight films — nine if we include *Elstree Calling* (1930), of which only a segment was by Hitchcock. None of these works came anywhere close to *The Lodger* in mood or signature or success, but perhaps this was to be expected. The director was trying not only to prolong his artistic self-invention but also to earn a living. He made melodramas and adaptations of plays, and was quite a long way from being able (or wanting) to concentrate on the thrillers we now associate with his name.

He also pioneered the shift to sound cinema for British International Pictures, making *Blackmail* (1929) first as a silent then a talking film. It's worth noting that throughout his career Hitchcock was loyal to certain styles and techniques of silent cinema at its best, which is why dialogue often disappears from his works for long stretches. He had no time for movies composed solely of what he called "photographs of people talking."

In his best early English films, Hitchcock concentrated on troubled, often violent relations between men and women. He also worked out a full-blown theory of suspense. When Truffaut said to him that "many people are under the impression that suspense is related to fear," Hitchcock sharply responded, "There is no relation whatever." He would go on to say, "In the usual form of suspense it is indispensable that the public be made perfectly aware of all of the facts involved." His example was a dinner party in a movie. In the first scenario, neither the watching audience nor the dinner guests know there is a bomb under the table, timed to go off in the near future. Nothing happens until the bomb goes off: surprise. In the second scenario, the audience knows about the bomb but the guests don't. Now we have suspense: The audience knows too much, we might say, but also not enough. It knows what will happen, but not quite what the reactions and results may be; and, of course, it is haunted by its knowledge of what the guests don't know. Or as Hitchcock put it, "Knowing what to expect, they [the audience] wait for it to happen." It can't be quite true that this waiting has "no relation whatever" to fear, but it isn't the same as fear or any kind of shock. And it has nothing to do with waiting for a mystery to be solved. The mystery is already solved — or displaced, situated in the midst of the story rather than at its end.

The Ring (1927) reaches its climax in a boxing match, which plays very carefully with what we know and can't yet know. One of these men will win (this is a movie; we can rule out a tie or an unfinished match), and we shall perhaps not be surprised in either case. As filmgoers we probably bet on the underdog — and we are right, as it happens. But will he keep his wife as well? She has been flirting quite openly with his rival for some scenes now. By the middle of the fight the underdog is doing really badly, and suddenly the woman's wandering affection reverts to him in his role as potential loser, not as conquering hero. This seems totally out of character and not where the movie was going. What's more, it's the sight of her changed face that revives him, allows him to find new energy and win the fight.

The Ring was shot by Jack Cox, who was the cameraman on

eleven Hitchcock films altogether. The visual invention is notable throughout, from the roller coaster shots at the beginning to the lighting of the fight at the end, but the most striking effects come with the very beautiful lingering close-ups on faces as their owners hesitate between thoughts. Hitchcock is right when he said, "In real life, people's faces don't reveal what they think or feel," and this opacity of character or intention recurs in his films. But as with so many of his shrewd pronouncements, we can accept the principle and also refine it a little. We can't tell exactly what the girl in *The Ring* is thinking, but we see in her face the conflict of the possibilities the plot has created for her, and we know that she is weighing her options, which involve both class and country. She is balancing the idea of a glamorous future with the gentleman Australian champion Bob against a modest happiness with the working-class English contender Jack, the two chances represented later in a Gypsy's pack of cards by the king of diamonds and the king of hearts. We don't know which way she is leaning, but neither does she, and the shot shows us that too.

In *Blackmail*, Alice has stabbed to death a man who was trying to rape her. When she leaves her attacker's flat she walks the streets of London all night, passing the tower of Big Ben and hearing the clock strike, seeing the lights of Piccadilly Circus. It's as if she had to take the city into her distraught confidence, make it a partner in her despair. Alice's policeman boyfriend, Frank, works out what she has done and is determined to keep her out of jail, but Alice doesn't want to escape or flee. She writes a note of confession — we see the shadows of bars across her face — and she goes to Scotland Yard to turn herself in. Frank keeps trying to persuade her to leave, yet she insists on staying; but a phone call to the commissioner interrupts their conversation and takes a while, so she finally lets herself be led away. This is where the film ends.

I used the word "rape" above. Other critics have spoken of "seduction" and "a fairly violent pass," and have suggested that killing the offending man is not the only way to preserve one's virtue. I agree with the scholar Tania Modleski that the act here is attempted rape, and that critics and viewers and indeed perhaps Hitchcock himself are too ready to shift the ground from male violence to female guilt — after all, they imply, Alice didn't have to go up to the man's room and flirt with him. Furthermore, the concept of attempted rape doesn't provide a simple justification of Alice's act, especially in her own view of what has happened. That's what makes her frame of mind so interesting. She is not a murderess but she has killed a man; the consequences of her instinctive response are hard to bear. They are what she carries around the London night with her.

Blackmail has a famous scene in which Hitchcock, taking an early opportunity with the medium, creates through sound the effect usually generated by images. A nosy neighbor of Alice's parents keeps gossiping about various notorious murders ("Pushed his lady-friends under the water while they were having a bath"), not knowing anything of what Alice has done. The neighbor thinks hitting your victim over the head with a brick is at least straightforward: "Something very British about that." As if her complete ignorance of Alice's act is a supersensory form of knowledge, she insists on her dislike of the knife as an instrument and repeats her preference for the brick. The sound track turns acutely subjective at this point and we begin to hear the woman's chatter through Alice's mind, the noise a figure for her disturbance, with the word "knife" isolated and coming up again and again like a refrain or an accusation. The joke about what is "British" is a minor element here, but it picks up a recurring motif in Hitchcock's films: The old country is not so much a historical place as a collection of lopsided dreams the natives have about the place.

Alice's situation produces the perfect Hitchcockian suspense. We know she has killed the man; we have all but seen
her do it, have certainly seen her step out from behind a curtain,
breadknife in hand. But then there is the characteristic double
move, as in *The Ring,* a double doubt: not just *Will she confess?,*
but *Will she keep trying if the confessing is interrupted?* And behind the suspense lies a perhaps unanswerable moral question,
which represents one of Hitchcock's enduring concerns. Here,
as in *Sabotage* (1936), we get to contemplate a killing that goes
unpunished. We feel an unmistakable relief at the fact that these
women have (so far) escaped the hands of the law; we have no
desire whatsoever for them to be caught. Almost simultane-
ously we also feel bad about our relief, because we have chosen
to betray justice and truth for the sake of a person who has committed an act of violence. Well, we haven't chosen — the film
has. But would we make such a choice? It's more comfortable to
think that justice and truth and the people we care about are all
on the same side.

Among the other films Hitchcock made for British International between 1927 and 1930, the most interesting, in a rather
perverse way, is *Murder!* (1930), and the plot again names a
woman as a killer. In this case she is only an accused killer, but
it is remarkable to find three films on this subject (*Blackmail,
Murder!,* and *Sabotage*) in a body of work whose fame rests so
firmly on the violence men do to women and whose first major
film is about a (male) serial killer.

The interest of *Murder!* is perverse because it belongs to the
genre that Hitchcock repeatedly said he didn't like, the English
mystery, centered on the corpse in the closed community. The
detective is Sir John Menier, expertly played by Herbert Marshall, who also appears in *Foreign Correspondent* (1940). Sir
John, an actor, is also an amateur sleuth of the supposed upper class, but given to terrible pontificating about his philoso-

phy and methods. The film isn't really a whodunit, except in its rather hollow structure. Our concern throughout—a brilliant displacement of emphasis on Hitchcock's part—is with the plight of Diana Baring, an actress who didn't do the murder but looks as if she did. Even Sir John, a doubting member of the jury, has gone along with the unanimous verdict. What's important is that no logic or restored causality can save Diana, nor can Sir John's laborious deductions. What saves her is Sir John's belief in her, and a certain bond between him and Diana as actors. She finally, reluctantly, mentions the killer's name— he was in love with her and also had a guilty social secret: He is a half-caste, although the tone and atmosphere of the story suggest that this is code for homosexuality. So we have an intriguing mirror version of the situation in *Blackmail:* In place of the guilty woman who wants to confess but doesn't, we have an innocent woman freed because she admits to having knowledge she would rather have kept to herself. Either way the law, and even the truth, becomes unreal or irrelevant, and the discovery of the actual murderer seems almost as accidental as the phone call in *Blackmail* that interrupts Alice's confession. This is a strange region of "England" certainly, but Hitchcock's England included many zones the establishment didn't care to contemplate.

In *Sabotage* as in *Blackmail* a guilty woman escapes at the end, and in the later film there could be no plea of self-defense. There are two terrorist attacks on London and we know who is behind them from the first. When Mr. Verloc (Oskar Homolka) returns home after the first venture—it has caused a blackout in a whole section of town—he picks up the newspaper but not to see the news. He knows the news. He wants the newspaper to cover his face while he takes a nap. For his second attempt he sends Stevie, his wife's young brother, off with a packet of explosives and two cans of film. Mr. Verloc, an agent not only of a sinister organization but also of several of Hitchcock's sardonic jokes, owns a cinema, the Bijou. In *Secret Agent,* the Joseph Conrad novel on which the movie is based, he runs a dubious bookshop purveying pornography and anarchist journals. The bomb of Hitchcock's illustration of suspense is quite literal here, even if the dinner party isn't. Indeed the film, as distinct from the Conrad novel from which Hitchcock borrows some of the characters and the bare framework of the action, gets a little too involved in the idea of delay, the baiting of our impeccable knowledge of what is to come. It's a fine touch that the boy Stevie is sent to plant the bomb in Piccadilly Circus on the day of the Lord Mayor's Show — a parade of soldiers, horses, and bands, with crowds everywhere in his way — but we didn't really need the toothpaste salesman who collars Stevie for his show, making the boy's lateness even more of a problem. A niggling reverse suspense begins to arise: When is Hitchcock going to stop playing with us? But then Stevie manages to take a bus, and we realize that neither he nor his fellow passengers are going to make it to their destination, and there is a truly brilliant and heartless sound dissolve from the exploding bus to an audience laughing in Mr. Verloc's cinema.

But if we know Stevie is to die, we don't know what his sister, Winnie, will do about his death or what will become of her. As soon as she hears of the explosion she understands what has happened and her husband's involvement in it. She keeps seeing Stevie's face among those of children on the street; she calls his name as if he could come to her help. And there is a remarkable scene in which she and Mr. Verloc sit at home and look at each other: slow zoom on her face; close-up on his; on hers; crosscutting between them. Finally she takes up a knife, that un-English instrument, and kills him. Then a fellow anarchist, anxious about what information may emerge when Verloc is caught, arrives and blows up the house with the body in it. But Winnie had already confessed to the police before the dynamiter arrived. The inspector seems to remember just this in the middle of all the excitement and confusion. "She said her husband was dead before the bomb went off." Then he decides he is not sure and pursues the matter no further. The mingling of bomb and uncertain memory is both more violent and subtler than the interrupting phone call in *Blackmail,* but it has the same effect. Winnie leaves England with her friend.

After Such Knowledge

The idea of war was everywhere during this period. The catchphrase applied to the 1914–1918 conflict — "the war to end all wars" — was one of those definitions that not only ask for trouble but also seem to contain the trouble they ask for. What that war meant to many people, especially in its notionally idealistic aftermath, was the promise that real war was just starting. The shell-shocked Septimus Smith of Virginia Woolf's *Mrs. Dalloway* (1925) had many real-life companions, and the notion of lies that we find in the poems both of Wilfred Owen and Ezra Pound was both new and prevalent. The "old lie" for Owen was the claim that dying in a war was gentle and proper, *dulce et decorum.* According to Pound, soldiers had "walked eye-deep in hell / believing in old men's lies," and had then, if they survived, come "home to a lie ... to old lies and new infamy." What was new here was the sense of a massive deception, of a whole nation being fed hypocritical fables — not about the war or the need for it, but about the human cost of the war and about who bore that cost. In this moral climate you didn't have to think about the war to be thinking about the war. Peace itself, with its distrust and uncertainty, followed by economic calamities later in the 1920s, was a war by other means, and no one was quite sure who the enemy was.

Hitchcock was affected by this climate like everyone else.

But he had an interest in the very idea of such a climate, and his social standing as an insider/outsider, a man who was perpetually insecure and able to give a terrific impersonation of security, no doubt helped to create for him a position that was both that of a player and of an audience member, a man who made things and liked to think about things.

Many of Hitchcock's titles glance at questions of knowledge: *Blackmail, Secret Agent, Young and Innocent* (released in America as *The Girl Was Young*), *Suspicion, Shadow of a Doubt, Notorious, I Confess, The Wrong Man*. Two of his films are called *The Man Who Knew Too Much*. The man in question there knows almost nothing, but this is still too much, since it is enough to place his little child in danger. In Hitchcock's films, it seems, there are only three options: to know too little, to know too much (however little that is), and to know a whole lot that is entirely plausible and completely wrong.

So to the idea of Hitchcock as an inventor we may add the idea of Hitchcock as a man exploring not so much our pursuit of knowledge as the reasons why it is so hard to come by. Had it always been hard to come by, and did this apply to all sorts of knowledge or just some? Hitchcock's films allow different answers to these questions, but they tilt us, I suggest, toward the belief that the interwar years offered something like a foundation for a new set of worries about knowledge, and that if some forms of knowledge were easier to get hold of, others were developing an almost magical resistance to inquiry. Examples of the first form would be news about the historical and political world, statistics, information about scientific progress, about ordinary life in other countries. Examples of the second would be comprehension of our friends' feelings or our own, assessments of guilt, motive, accountability, of the very idea of curiosity and its risks. We not only moved into an information age with the rise of newspapers and celebrities, but we began more than ever to need an education in what to believe and how to believe — an education in interpretation, let's say. I don't think Hitchcock set out to provide us with this education, or with any education at all. He wanted to entertain us, amuse himself, and become as rich as he could. But that precisely, as it happens, is how he gave us our education. If we'd thought it was an education, we wouldn't have paid attention.

By 1934 Hitchcock had returned to work with Michael Balcon, now at Gaumont-British, and he made the best known and most enduring of his British films for this company — the exception being *The Lady Vanishes* (1938), a wonderful film made for Gainsborough. He was now not only the most famous British film director, internationally well regarded, but he was also the only director who was a sort of star. Otherwise, movie audiences thought only of actors, and perhaps even, as Federico Fellini once said of himself as a young man, believed they made up their lines and directed themselves.

Hitchcock had also become, and would always remain, rather large in the physical sense. He was merely plump as a boy, and there are pictures of him as a young man where he looks almost slim. But by the time of a well-known photograph taken during the shooting of *The 39 Steps,* he looks huge; the paunch is considerable and the face has filled out a lot. His expression is rather contented, but there is maybe a faint flicker of apprehension in his face. This photographer has perhaps caught him a little off his guard. In other photographs there's a hint of temporary annoyance or perhaps a more enduring grumpiness. Sometimes the grumpiness seems closer to scorn. Certain photographs clean up or stylize this effect. Hitchcock looks soulful, slightly quizzical — a portrait of the artist as an artist. There is sorrow in the face, but also something like speculation. And resignation, the look of a man who knows you can't always have what you want. In other photographs he has the air of a bystander, just a stout, accidental fellow, hands in his pockets, a slight grimace on his face, a slight frown. He certainly dieted from time to time — dieted all the time, if champagne and steak were a diet — and lost large numbers of pounds, only to gain them again. It's easy to speculate about what this corpulence meant to him, and he liked to joke about his shape being a sexual hindrance. But was this a dark painful joke papering over distress, or just a way of getting people off his stomach?

All of Hitchcock's major films of the 1930s portray, with great care, a curious mixture of national habits and international affairs, brilliantly tangled in a running joke in *The Lady Vanishes*. Two rather stuffy gentlemen, leftovers from some clubby Edwardian world, wonderfully played by Basil Radford and Naunton Wayne, worry about England. The time is roughly the time of the film itself, and they are stranded on a train in the Balkans, notionally on their way home. Their concern seems justified. A newspaper headline they have seen says "England on the Brink." One of them tries to console the other by saying, "The old country's been in some tight corners before." The movie runs for quite a while before we realize that for these men "England" is the name not of the country at large but of the national cricket team. They are wondering how their side is doing against Australia, and whether the delayed train will get them home in time for the next test match.

Hitchcock's personal world did not include much, if any, cricket, even as a spectator sport. But he knew the shorthand the game represented, and he understood, as all English people do, the system of signs known as class. He knew, for example, that cricketers were divided into players (professionals) and gentlemen (amateurs). Above all he knew that sports, or rather a certain attitude toward sports, the notion of playing the game, was according to some English fantasies the peculiar possession of the English ruling classes. You couldn't expect subalterns, or

Frenchmen, or the English lower orders, to get the hang of it. In this view, to take "England" as the name of a cricket team was not a narrow approach: idealistic, rather — the implication of a hope that the country's noblest aspect might stand for the rest. When Margaret Lockwood's character in *The Lady Vanishes* dismisses "a thing like cricket" as entirely trivial, the splutter and the facial expressions of our two clubmen are themselves a sort of national anthem, a defense of an outraged empire.

This world, or this fantasy about a world, had not died when Hitchcock started making movies, but it was certainly ailing and easily ridiculed. Yet Hitchcock was a patriot in his dissenting way, and England meant many things to him. We might add that the stuffy gentlemen turn out to be good chaps to have on your side in a shoot-out, and that one of the enemy conspirators refuses to help kill a victim because she and the victim are both English. "England" means class and idiotic prejudices, but also a certain solidarity and a sense of proportion even in the midst of violence. When Robert Donat, in *The 39 Steps,* finds himself making an impromptu political speech, he appeals for "a square deal and a sporting chance" and is rapturously applauded. It is true he is supposed to be Canadian and he is in Scotland, but England goes a long way in the movies.

Risk Management

"It was purely a coincidence," Hitchcock said, tongue firmly in cheek, "that three of my films in succession . . . should all have a background of spying . . ." He added that *Sabotage,* which he was then making, "is a straightforward criminal thriller, without a spy in it." Without a spy but with a network of international terrorists. Killing in these works is no longer the largely private matter it was in the earlier films. With *The Man Who Knew Too*

Much, death and death threats become inextricably entangled in political, often international plots. But what kind of politics is in question? By 1938 the politics are of appeasement. The Nazis are hard at work conspiring to take over the world and the English are worrying about cricket. This is the inane version of national innocence. Or to put that more kindly, those who do not wish to oppose force with force are hoping for the best. The German occupation of Czechoslovakia provoked not the outbreak of war but the Munich Agreement. But in 1934 the politics of the films were more diffuse, based on a sense of entanglement in a world that was very poorly understood. What was clear was that the entanglement itself could not be avoided, that any idea of Britain as an island in anything other than a geographical sense was becoming more and more delusional.

In *The Man Who Knew Too Much* English accents, jokes, and manners begin to look like forms of ineptness rather than marks of a comfortable ruling class. Also forms of isolation. When a child is kidnapped to prevent its parents from passing on a secret they have picked up in Switzerland — the film begins with a litter of brochures promoting foreign travel — they don't see why anyone else should worry about a threat from someone they have never heard of. The MI5 man who is talking to them says, "Tell me, in June 1914 had you ever heard of a place called Sarajevo till a certain day in 1914?"

The plot the parents have learned of involves the assassination of a foreign diplomat at the Royal Albert Hall, the scene of a great Hitchcock set piece involving a vast choir and orchestra playing music by Arthur Benjamin, a clash of cymbals and a shriek from the child's mother that saves the diplomat's life. And then Hitchcock adds some domestic historical material to complement his international theme: His version of the siege of Sidney Street. This occurred in 1911, not far from where the Hitchcocks lived. A gang of burglars with political affiliations and aspirations, led by one Peter Piatkow, whose other identities historians are still trying to settle, holed up in a house and tried to fight off the police. The battle lasted more than six hours, and then home secretary Winston Churchill called in a detachment of the Scots Guards to help the police. The building caught fire, gang members died, and so did policemen and a fireman.

In the film, two policemen die because they try to rush the building and others die in the shoot-out. All the gang members die, although for a moment it seems as though the leader, played by Peter Lorre with a curious, smiling sinister ease, may get away, as his historical forebear did. The dialogue reminds us that these are not ordinary burglars. When the chief marksman says he thinks he'll leave, he is firmly told, "You took this on for our cause and you've got to go through with it." The cause is not named, and in one sense it is a simple plot device like the activity of the group known as the Thirty-Nine Steps, a means of putting someone in danger and creating the need for a rescue or a release. But the device itself signifies. Here as in *Sabotage* natives and foreigners are up to something the authorities have to squash. England is the not-quite-passive scene of international affairs. And even the approach to passivity looks like a luxury or a mistake, a form of weakness on which conspirators can rely.

The entanglement with the foreign continues in *The 39 Steps* (1935), although it is entirely unintentional on the part of the main character. When a lady with a mysterious European accent (Lucie Mannheim) tells the hero of the movie that she fired two shots in a theater to create a diversion, he says casually that it "sounds like a spy story." That's because it is one, but our hero, Richard Hannay (Robert Donat), is not going to understand this for a while — not until she is killed, in fact.

Then he gets it. A group of enemy agents is plotting to ship a crucial secret out of the country, and "it is only a matter of days, perhaps hours," his unfortunate informant tells him, be-

fore this will happen. Hannay, suspected of her murder, takes
off for Scotland and a whole series of adventures, meeting up
with Pamela (Madeleine Carroll), which is lucky for him and
the movie, since there is a lot of wooden, unamusing acting from
Donat and some rickety plotting all around, and she brings life
to everything that otherwise looks limp. Even with her, this film
seems like a good idea rather than a good movie — except for
two magnificent moments.

The first is the one everybody remembers, and one that has
had many disturbing historical echoes, notably in the case of
Konstantin Volkov, a Russian defector in Istanbul in 1945 who
would have had so much to say to British intelligence. He didn't
say anything because the man sent out to debrief him was Kim
Philby, a senior figure in MI6 and also a Russian agent. The
would-be informant was never heard of again.

Hannay knows very little about what he is doing or where
he is going, but he has learned that the leader of the enemy
group, a man who possesses a dozen names and can be a thousand persons, has one distinguishing feature he cannot alter: He
is missing a piece of a finger on one hand. After much scram-
bling about on the Scottish moors, taking refuge with a crofter
and narrowly escaping various pursuers, Hannay arrives at a
large country house where he expects to be able to deliver his
warning about the secret to the appropriate authority. His host
is very welcoming, and Hannay tells him his full story, including the supposed means of identifying the enemy. He is said to
have a piece of one finger missing. The genial host says, "Which
one?" Hannay holds up his hand to demonstrate: "This one, I
think." The host says, "Sure it wasn't this one?," and we see a
close-up of a hand with a piece of a finger missing.

The other great scene in the movie has a different valence.
The secret to be transported out of the country is being stored
in an unusual place: in the mind of a music-hall performer

called Mr. Memory. Mr. Memory recalls everything—football results, racing winners, historical landmarks—and has been asked to memorize the secret stuff for the spies. He doesn't ask questions about this; he's just proud of his memory and glad of the job. He has even memorized a definition of the Thirty-Nine Steps and recites it: "an organization of spies collecting information on behalf of the foreign service of . . ." At this point— we are close to the end of the film now and taking in a second performance by Mr. Memory, at the Palladium this time, and we have seen the man with the missing piece of finger in the audience—he is shot and doesn't complete his sentence. He does manage, though, before he dies, to recite the whole secret, with great pride in his prowess. He says, "Am I right, sir?," which is his catchword with any answer in his show. And then, more personally, "I'm glad it's off my mind." There's a certain figure of Englishness here, not unlike that of the butler Stevens in Kazuo Ishiguro's *The Remains of the Day*. Mr. Memory is glad it's off his mind because it was taking up space there, and no doubt because he didn't like being the carrier of such treasonous stuff. But his mind was not made for thinking, and he was just doing his job. "The whole idea," Hitchcock told Truffaut, "is that the man is doomed by his sense of duty . . . [W]hen he is asked the question, he is *compelled* to give the answer. The schoolteacher in *The Birds* dies for the same reason." These deaths are touching and in their way admirable—Hitchcock told the biographer Charlotte Chandler that Mr. Memory was one of his favorite characters. But they also belong to a blinkered old order of submission. A certain deviation from duty, in Hitchcock, is often the way to salvation.

The time frame of these films involving spies, anarchists, assassins, and conspiracies is quite ample. The siege of Sidney Street, as we have seen, puts us in 1911. *The 39 Steps* is based on a John Buchan novel of the same name that first appeared in 1915.

And *The Lady Vanishes* brings the Nazis into the picture, so we must be in the later 1930s — the date of the first screening of the film is 1938, also the year of the Munich Agreement.

The implication, if we put together these real and imaginary dates, is quite consistent. England is at risk, in wartime and peacetime, and scarcely knows it; and if it knew, it would be inclined to ignore or underestimate the threat. The point is not directly historical or political, and of course Hitchcock is not inviting us to leave the world of entertainment, or the pleasure of imaginary dangers, in order to doggedly worry about the real ones. The real ones, in any case, are more diffuse and complicated and don't all have to do with reprehensible foreign bad guys or their agents. But entertainment, especially when it is as intelligently orchestrated as it is by Hitchcock, can have a historical and political import, and this is seen throughout *The Lady Vanishes*.

Here is a friendly, eccentric, old English lady, played by Dame May Whitty, who seems to have been borrowed from Agatha Christie but placed in the wrong story. She's a spy, not an amateur detective, and her name, Miss Froy, bears a resemblance to Freud's. She's a reader of signs, of what's hidden in the terrible song sung outside her window at a Balkans hotel, for example; she gets the secret message without even knowing that the singer has been killed for including it in his song. There is also a young couple in the movie, played by Michael Redgrave and Margaret Lockwood, who finally strike the note Hitchcock has been seeking for some time, perhaps since he started in the movies: that of people who can banter, even be rude to each other, but never lose their charm or give up their mutual attraction, never divert us from the sense that they belong together.

Above all we find in this movie the fable that we saw in *The 39 Steps* and that brings into focus all Hitchcock's stories of misplaced trust and wandering suspicion; the fable, that is, of the archenemy whom you take to be your best friend. Here the couple, Gilbert (Redgrave) and Iris (Lockwood), searching for the mysteriously vanished Miss Froy, think everyone is against them except the polite and plausible doctor played by the Hungarian actor Paul Lukas. He is called Hartz and sounds German, although he says he comes from Prague — a small difference, as it happens, since by 1938 Czechoslovakia had been annexed by Germany — but as the film scholar Karen Beckman suggests in her book *Vanishing Women: Magic, Film, and Feminism,* the displacement "avoids overt typecasting of the German as a villain." Gilbert and Iris certainly don't do any such typecasting. They are right to think that pretty much everyone is lying to them when they say they haven't seen any lady resembling Miss Froy, but wrong, alas, not to guess that these people are all lying at Dr. Hartz's behest, that he is the mastermind behind the disappearance. He doesn't have a piece of his finger missing, but when he reveals himself as a German agent he begins to bark nasty orders, and we realize what it is that has taken in Gilbert and Iris. Dr. Hartz is authoritative, but has until now been exceptionally civil — a classy type, one of them. In Hitchcock the Nazis don't strut about and salute; they inhabit elegant drawing rooms, they are often English or American, and they are indistinguishable in manner from their rich friends. Until they start talking politics or taking over the action.

The sociologist T. W. Adorno, not a superstitious man, had his version of the saying that even paranoids have enemies, writing in *Minima Moralia:* "Psychology knows that he who imagines disasters in some way desires them. But why do they come so eagerly to meet him?" Adorno goes on to say he feels he should have been able to predict the rise of fascism from the behavior of his schoolmates in Germany. He didn't, but his shock was not complete. "The outbreak of the Third Reich did, it is true, surprise my political judgement, but not my unconscious fear." Hitchcock would say you didn't have to go to school in Germany to have such fears. He would also say — did say through his conspiracy movies — that the English failure to have such fears, or the failure to have enough of them, had become a defining feature of national identity.

3

Atlantic Crossings

Perfect Symmetry

THE HITCHCOCKS VISITED America in 1937 and made a big splash in New York City and Hollywood: movie royalty on tour. They had a good time too, and McGilligan tells us that "Hitchcock was already dreaming of America" as early as 1932. If Germany was the home of much of what the movies meant visually to him (it had once been the center of the industry), Hollywood was now the world capital of film, and Hitchcock's ambitions led him to look away from the provinces toward the metropolis. However, it was March 1939 when he (and Alma and Pat and his secretary Joan Harrison) set sail, a few months before the European war broke out.

Hitchcock had by this time signed a contract with David O. Selznick, and his first job was to direct *Rebecca* for Selznick International Pictures. He had stayed in England a little longer than he meant to in order to finish *Jamaica Inn,* starring Charles Laughton and based on a novel of the same name by Daphne du Maurier. Hitchcock took on only one costume drama after this, the disappointing (especially to him) *Under Capricorn* (1949), but this first excursion at least, in hindsight, has the enormous benefit of Laughton's unapologetic overacting.

The Hitchcocks rented a house from Carole Lombard and later bought a house on Bellagio Road in Bel Air. There is a characteristic story about the purchase. Alma found the house and was very excited; Hitchcock pretended not to be inter-

ested, and then owlishly gave her the key to the place as a birthday present. She probably didn't like such tricks any more than
he did when he wasn't playing them, but she loved the house,
and they stayed there for the rest of their lives, making additions
and alterations as they went along. Pat attended Marymount
High School in Los Angeles, became very keen on drama, and
by 1942 had a small part in a play on Broadway. When she grad-
uated she became a student at the Royal Academy of Dramatic
Art in London and later appeared in three of her father's movies, most notably *Strangers on a Train*. She also appeared in ten
episodes of Hitchcock's first television series and edited the
books associated with those programs.

Hitchcock's situation with David Selznick was rather
strange. He was under contract, but his boss kept loaning him
out to other producers and studios, so that in the end he made
only three films for Selznick over seven years. After *Rebecca,*
Hitchcock made one film for Walter Wanger, three for RKO,
two for Universal, and one for Fox, returning to Selznick for
Spellbound (1945) and *The Paradine Case* (1947). Hitchcock
complained about the financial arrangement — the large chunk
of his earnings that Selznick was entitled to — and was relieved
to be away from the great man's interfering gaze. The mutual experience with *Rebecca* had not been a happy one, and perhaps
caused Hitchcock to think less well of this film than he might
otherwise have done.

Claude Chabrol and Eric Rohmer call *Rebecca* a crime genre
fairy tale, *un conte de fées policier,* and the opening certainly
strikes a dark and magical note. It's all quotation from the novel.
"Last night I dreamt I went to Manderley again," Mrs. de Winter (Joan Fontaine) says in a strange, singsongy tone, as if she
were reading a story to a child or reciting a poem for a teacher.

It seemed to me I stood by the iron gate leading to the drive, and
for a while I could not enter, for the way was barred to me . . .

Then, like all dreamers, I was possessed of a sudden with supernatural powers and passed like a spirit through the barrier before
me . . . On and on wound the poor thread that had once been our
drive . . .

But since this is a film we see what she is talking about. It
doesn't look like a dream at all; it looks like a real, shifting picture of a dark and tangled wood. The supernatural powers seem
to belong to the camera rather than the character, and the images suggest a troubled mind. And then the images, rather than
depicting the memory of a cherished place, actually begin to
contradict the voice. "Time could not mar the perfect symmetry of those walls," Mrs. de Winter says, and we peer through
the trees at a black and jagged ruin, a Gothic scramble of tur-
rets and mullioned windows. It's beautiful but it's too confusing
to evoke anything like perfect symmetry. It may just be that the
set designer got carried away, but the effect is wonderful. It is in
keeping with the tone of the voice, if not with what the voice is
saying. Is it possible to betray a book by sheer fidelity to it?

It turns out that this very question came up between the
producer and the director. "It's not a Hitchcock picture," the director said. He was wrong but in a rather complicated way. It
was certainly called a "David O. Selznick film," and when it won
an Oscar for Best Picture the credit went to Selznick. Hitchcock was nominated for Best Director but John Ford won that
prize for *The Grapes of Wrath,* another film based on a novel.
Perhaps Selznick's idea of fidelity had something to do with it.
"We bought *Rebecca,*" Selznick wrote in a memo objecting to a
first draft of the screenplay, "and we intend to make *Rebecca.*"
"We" in this instance was Selznick. But then there is so much of
what we now think of as Hitchcock in the film that we wonder
why he would want to disavow it. Because there wasn't enough?
Because he saw more Selznick than there really was?

Late in the film Maxim de Winter (Laurence Olivier), Mrs.

de Winter's husband, says she no longer has the "lost, funny look" she used to have, which may be true, but she has shed it only temporarily. The voice tells us — and in this it is quite unlike the voice in the novel whose words it often uses — that looking back on her story she is as lost as she always was, and understands what has happened to her as little as she ever did. Fontaine conveys this effect visually as well as aurally. She has an odd, veiled, intermittently recurring gaze that converts her frank and often beautiful face into a mask of near idiocy, as if she is not only innocent but also not quite right in the head.

Hitchcock was not very enthusiastic about Fontaine, even though he did direct two fine movies with her as his star. Perhaps she was too serious, or scared, and she certainly didn't like Hitchcock's rough and rude jokes. Alma and others of the director's associates thought she was "coy and simpering." In any case, his recollections have none of the kind words for her that he reserved for Ingrid Bergman and Grace Kelly, who were both favorites and friends, and regularly appear in photographs with him where the sense of warmth and hilarity is almost tangible. Perhaps because of Hitchcock's lack of praise, critics have often undervalued Fontaine's performances, even if she received an Oscar nomination for *Rebecca* and won an Oscar for *Suspicion*. This scanting is a pity, because she gets remarkable effects in both films. Her character is or becomes slightly crazy each time, and yet she retains her sweet, intelligent appearance. A sort of disassociation occurs, and it's very haunting. The biographer Donald Spoto's phrase "muted disquiet" is helpful. In *Rebecca*, Fontaine's character is lost but doesn't know how lost she is, so it's as if her own bewilderment was not quite accessible to her. In *Suspicion,* she's not lost but actively deluded, yet still has the same polite, diligent look of a woman who is tidying up her life, even if it involves suspecting her husband of planning murder.

It's a good thing Mrs. de Winter continues to be lost in *Rebecca,* since Maxim de Winter married her as a naive little girl in the South of France, and the last thing he wants is a relationship with a grown-up woman. He's already been married to one of those, the glamorous and unfaithful Rebecca, and it looks at one point as if he killed her. That's why he's brooding over the memory of her drowning, not, as we are at first invited to believe, because he can't get over his bereavement. In his book of interviews with Hitchcock, Truffaut says he has "never completely understood" the actual explanation of Rebecca's death. Hitchcock patiently replies: "Well, the explanation is that Rebecca wasn't killed by her husband; she committed suicide because she had cancer." Truffaut says he got that, but still wonders whether the husband may not believe himself to be guilty in some way. Hitchcock says crisply: "No, he doesn't."

As far as the film is concerned Truffaut had the right worry, but about the wrong person. Of course the girl-wife thinks Maxim has killed Rebecca, because at one point he seems precisely to say so; and the viewer has been thinking this all along. We know the genre by now. If it's not the madwoman in the attic it's the corpse in the ocean. Jane Eyre and her many literary children fall in love only with hampered, guilty men. But then Hitchcock, it turns out, is playing with just these expectations. Maxim de Winter is not the dark romantic villain we and his new wife hankered for and thought we knew. He's just a sullen, spoiled fellow who had a bad marriage.

After their wedding Maxim and his new wife drive through the grounds of Manderley in an open-top car. We look back toward them, seeing them through the windshield; we see them in close-up from the side. Then it starts to rain. Fontaine puts a raincoat over her head, and Hitchcock suddenly reverses the angle. We see the backs of the protagonists in close-up: her hooded head, his coat and hat. Then the house appears, a gleaming pile in the pouring rain, our vision crossed by the movement of the wipers. The change in the weather, which looked for a moment like a rather literary portent of unhappiness, now seems to suggest something unapproachable about the house itself, as if it will always hide behind a screen, literal or metaphorical.

This is fine stuff, and far from "picturization," but there is a sequence that is even more striking. The newlyweds are watching a home movie of their honeymoon, all rather sickly and sweet and out of character — well, out of his character. They are interrupted by the news of one of Mrs. de Winter's many gaffes in her role as mistress of the house. Upon getting back to their viewing, she offends him by casually using the word "gossip" in relation to his past. Hitchcock chooses to picture them both in the dark, her face lit by the flickering light from the screen, his lit by what remains of the light when he steps in front of the projector and blocks the cheerful film from us and her. She looks like the victim of an interrogation, and he looks like someone who has wandered in from the set of *Nosferatu* or *The Cabinet of Dr. Caligari:* In one shot, the light falls sideways across his face in such a way as to make him seem to have only one eye. His wavy, brilliantined hair and military mustache, along with his harsh gaze, suggest some sort of rigid court-martial of the sexes. What is going on here? It certainly isn't just the little conjugal misunderstanding the plot and dialogue have laid out for us. It is a kind of visual fairy tale and one very much of Hitchcock's making. It is the story of the ogre and the little girl, in which she loves him because he may kill her, and he accepts her (and doesn't kill her) because he loves her fear. That's why they can live happily ever after — as long as she doesn't recognize the Gothic mansion of his appetite for what it is.

Once in a Lifetime

Rebecca was the first of what Hitchcock called the two "English" films he made in America. The second was *Suspicion* (1941).

Both were based on novels by English writers, had English actors in them, and displayed what Hitchcock thought of as an English "atmosphere." More important, both inhabited what I will call the shadow of Jack the Ripper, or if you prefer of Hitchcock's own film *The Lodger*.

Hitchcock loved the Ripper story, and yet returned to it more as a foil than a fact, the wrong version that tempted everyone. Of course, if it wasn't tempting it wouldn't do the work it was asked to do, and this is what Hitchcock understood so well. He might have taken his motto from a fragmentary poem by the naturalized Englishman T. S. Eliot, who knew a lot about these regions of the imagination and about the popular theater world that Hitchcock so often evoked. In Eliot's *Sweeney Agonistes* one of the characters tells us that he "knew a man once did a girl in," adding that "any man" might want to do the same thing, indeed that "any man has to, needs, wants to" do it, at least "once in a lifetime."

The casual murky generalizing is very fast, and "once in a lifetime" is (in context) curiously modest. We note too that the woman is a girl, and that the idiom of "doing in" discreetly distances the act into slang, as if it were a folk habit of the speakers of this language, nothing as crude as killing or murder. Hitchcock is not quite as jocular as this — although often pretty jocular all the same — but these are his registers of speculation. What might a man do? What might he persuade himself that he needs to do? And what is the relation of "any man" to the men who do these things?

The credits of *Suspicion* arise over a postcard-style picture of rural England: trees, fields, a cottage. This conventional scenery shows up throughout the film and is especially associated with the end of the village where Isobel Sedbusk (Auriol Lee), the supposedly celebrated writer of crime stories, lives. This is the semi-imaginary England where so many murder mysteries are set, the small community where everyone knows everyone, but the solution to the mystery is supposed to be a surprise. We can see why Hitchcock thought of this American film as English; even more clearly than in *Rebecca,* perhaps, we grasp what he meant by an English atmosphere.

In the novel the film is based on, *Before the Fact* by Francis Iles (the nom de plume of Anthony Berkeley), the husband is a murderer, and the wife is so crazily in love with him she is going to allow him to kill her. Hitchcock and many critics suggest that changes were forced upon him by Hollywood decorum and Cary Grant's refusal to play a murderer. And by a calculation about audience response: No one would want Grant to be a murderer or believe he was. The situation thus exactly mirrors the reported situation of *The Lodger:* dark plot trivially lightened by the star system. I don't doubt that such pressure was in play, even a major motive for changes. What I doubt, here as with *The Lodger,* is that in the end Hitchcock got anything other than just what he wanted, namely a wonderfully realized world of uncertain knowledge, where suspicion will never be enough and never go away, even when the supposed happy end has been declared.

What is magnificent in *Suspicion* is the way the film can unsettle anything. We might think that the crisscrossing pressures I have just described would produce a kind of standoff between the dark original and the light translation — not a whodunit but an unanswerable *Is he planning to do it?* But in any careful viewing of the film we are likely to replace the will-he-or-won't-he question with a related but more frightening one: How can she be thinking what she is thinking, and will she ever get over it? We might even ask a similar question to the one raised by the Iles novel. Does she love her husband too much not to fear the worst about him? Is she partly in love with that very worst possibility?

Fontaine plays Lina McLaidlaw, a mousy young woman who seems to have been both neglected and oppressed by her elderly parents, the father a military man, the mother a submissive wife. She is beautiful, because this is a movie and she is Joan Fontaine, and she is intelligent and brave, and has a wonderful way of lifting one eyebrow when surprised, but she is mousy all the same. She falls in love with Johnnie Aysgarth, a man-about-the-country played by Cary Grant, who foxhunts, goes to all the parties, and has all the girls hanging around him. To her and our surprise he falls for her too and marries her.

The marriage is a series of surprises for Lina. The couple returns from the honeymoon (Naples, Monte Carlo, Venice, Paris) to a palatial pad in the English countryside, with room after sumptuously furnished room, and a polite, curtseying maid to boot. Lina says Johnnie will have "to go to work" to support this lifestyle. The idea occasions much mirth and evasion on his part. "I've been broke all my life," he says, and his idea of how to get hold of money is to "borrow some more."

Johnnie gets a job, or seems to, managing estates. But then Lina's father dies and Johnnie's days of toil seem to be over, or to put it more unkindly, his marital expectations seem to have been met. But then Lina's father leaves her only a tiny annuity. Oh, and a ghastly large painting of the general in uniform. There is a moment here when the whole inference of the movie may be decided, for us if not for Lina. As the will is read out and he learns of the legacy, Johnnie goes into the neighboring room and pours himself a drink. In a very nice touch, he tops it off before he has even had a sip. When the pickings are slim you need to pick all you can. This is the room where the painting of the general currently hangs. Johnnie raises his glass to the painting, salutes, and says, "You win, old boy." On the principle that anyone can do anything, there is no prediction we can make based on this scene. We might plausibly guess, however, that such a stylish loser is unlikely to be a murderer. It is true that Lina doesn't have the benefit of this particular insight into her husband's character.

Johnnie has a friend called Beaky, a stereotypically blithering English idiot, cheerily played by Nigel Bruce as if he was repeating his portrait of Watson from the Sherlock Holmes movies he did with Basil Rathbone. Beaky has an awkward, plot-driven medical condition that means a full glass of brandy may kill him off. We see him spluttering and helpless when he serves himself too liberally early in the movie. Later he dies in Paris after drinking a large glass of brandy. An unidentified English friend was with him at the time. Could this have been Johnnie? He stood to make a lot of money from Beaky's death because of a development scheme they had set up together. Beaky was having second thoughts, insofar as he was capable of thought, and his death cut them off. But Johnnie wasn't in Paris. Or was he? When Lina learns of Beaky's death she suspects Johnnie — because doing your old pal out of his money is the same sort of thing as killing him, especially if you have to kill him to do him out of his money — and calls his club in London. He's not there. Lina tries to tell herself — and does tell her father's portrait — that "he didn't go to Paris." But she keeps courting the very theory she is trying to deny, and Johnnie's return doesn't convince her of his innocence, nor does his manifest affection for Beaky or his distress at the old boy's death.

From here on the film speeds to its climax. Lina's suspicion converts itself into a certainty. We focus on a glass of milk that Lina believes is poisoned and that does indeed look a little strange — because Hitchcock has placed a lightbulb in it. But how could we *see* the poison? It wouldn't make the milk glow — only suspicion does that.

We witness a hair-raising car ride along the cliffs, crashing sea below seen from a high angle, the whole take lifted from *Re-*

becca and later borrowed by Olivier for Hamlet's soliloquy. The car door swings open, and Johnnie seems to be pushing Lina out. But no, he's trying to keep her in, to stop her from falling. He realizes what she has been thinking and why she has been treating him so strangely; she understands how completely her fiction has carried her away.

At this point Hitchcock performs a small movie miracle. We see the car, with its open top, from the back, and as it starts to move, Johnnie's arm falls around Lina's shoulders. This is a kindly, protective embrace, of course, a confirmation of the happy end. He has just saved her life. Now is not the moment to start suspecting him. But we do. Or I do. There is something threatening about the falling arm, its claiming of possession. And yet it remains true that nothing supports Lina's suspicion except her suspicion. With the menace in the arm Hitchcock is just insinuating a little disarray into what was supposed to be a resolution.

Gone with the Wind

Hitchcock made two American films between *Rebecca* and *Suspicion: Foreign Correspondent* (1940) and *Mr. & Mrs. Smith* (1941). The latter was a brave excursion into American screwball comedy starring Carole Lombard and Robert Montgomery, which was pretty funny but rather slow compared with the native classics of the genre. The former was plodding work for a lot of the time, but it led Hitchcock right into the troubled topic of the war in the world he had left behind.

Hitchcock was much reviled for leaving England at the beginning of the war, or rather a few months before it began. He was, like W. H. Auden and Christopher Isherwood, reviled at home for staying abroad. By August 1940 Michael Balcon, his old friend and employer, was sneering at "famous directors" hiding out in Hollywood while others contributed to the war effort in a country under attack. One of his articles in the *Sunday Dispatch* in 1940 was entitled "Deserters." Other locals joined the chorus, and the actor Seymour Hicks suggested the production of a film called *Gone with the Wind Up,* starring Charles Laughton and Herbert Marshall, and directed by Hitchcock.

Strangely, even the call for American support that Hitchcock inserted into his film *Foreign Correspondent* ("Hello, America, hang on to your lights, they're the only lights left in the world") did not go down well at home. It was taken as an insult to the sturdy British, an insinuation that they couldn't manage on their own. Actually, as McGilligan tells us, a few members of the British colony in Hollywood did return to England to take up military service. Hitchcock made several trips back during the war, offering contributions of different kinds to wartime causes and directing two films in support of the Free French. At the end of the war, he worked on a full-length film made up of documentary footage of the German concentration camps.

Still, there are questions here. The accusations against Hitchcock were overheated and unfair — he was not a "deserter" from any army, even a metaphorical one — but we may feel that his presence in England as a director would have made a difference to the national mood and economy, apart from any propaganda in the films themselves. In wartime, as in other times, quality is a kind of morale. I am taking my cue from an excellent article by film professor Charles Barr, which is where I also found the suggestion that the Hitchcocks' decision to stay in America was largely based on personal and professional, even financial, considerations for their own future that Alfred and Alma placed before their debt to their country. This is a reasonable choice, and only real heroes can have a quarrel with it, as distinct from the heroes we all imagine we might be.

Foreign Correspondent was created from a property that had been knocking around Hollywood for some time looking for a writer and a director. It was a memoir about the 1920s by Vincent Sheean, an American newsman who had worked in many places abroad. Alma Hitchcock and Joan Harrison devised a treatment, and Hitchcock brought in Charles Bennett, an old friend and collaborator, to turn the thing into a script. Robert Benchley, who had an amiable, meandering part in the movie as the sort of foreign correspondent who doesn't do anything, said the film turned into "an out-and-out melodrama like *The Lady Vanishes* or *The 39 Steps,* only not so good."

In many ways the film is even worse than that sounds. It's not really a melodrama; it's a spy thriller mixed with a timid screwball comedy, and Hitchcock's heart plainly wasn't in it. He was rumored to be drinking a pint of champagne at lunch every day and sleeping through most of the shooting. He weighed three hundred pounds — "an all-time peak," McGilligan says. Much of the film is genuinely inept. Maybe there is a way of dreaming things in as well as phoning them in.

But then the film wakes up, or finds its way. Our hero, John Jones (Hitchcock wanted Gary Cooper but got Joel McCrea), is sent to London to find out what's happening with the war — the war that has started in Europe but is only about to start in the film's narrative time. John witnesses an assassination — this is the first moment at which the film comes alive, the setting a rainy day in a Dutch city, all umbrellas and impressive town hall steps — which turns out to be a trick. A look-alike has been killed, and the real target has been kidnapped for torturing until he reveals the secret the enemies of peace want to know. It's not quite clear who these enemies are — their chief is the London ambassador to a place called Borovia — although they have to be Germans in the end. The chief reason we know they are enemies is that they go on about peace so much, while casually having people killed off. The impeccable Herbert Marshall plays

Stephen Fisher, the head of this gang, who has managed to deceive even his daughter, Carol (Laraine Day), about his politics. She falls in love with John and gets caught between two men and two very different views of the world. Much tricky and silly plotting helps to keep this story going, although we do have the pleasure of seeing George Sanders show up in one of his rare roles (his only role?) as a cheery good guy, Scott ffolliott. Even more than John, Scott is the man who outs the conspirators. John, as befits his job, gets the news across.

Stephen and Carol Fisher make their escape from Europe on a plane headed to America. Suddenly the plane is attacked by a German destroyer, starts to fall apart, and ultimately crashes into the ocean. There are few survivors. This was bravura filming for the time, involving nose-diving photos from within a plane, a vast studio tank, smashed glass, forlorn figures stranded on a separated wing. Before the attack, though, in a curiously moving scene, Stephen confesses to his daughter. He has been loyal to his country, he says, but his country is not England, and he has been loyal in what he calls "a very difficult way." "Sometimes," he adds, "it's harder to fight dishonorably than nobly in the open." He insists that he is not going to say anything of the kind to his judges, only wants his daughter to know that he feels "a little ashamed." He doesn't formally say what his country is — presumably she knows. She is shocked and is not about to defend him or agree with him. But she begins to understand him and he is her father.

A little later, when they are out on the broken wing of the plane, an argument occurs about taking on a survivor, the pilot, who swims to them from the wreck. A member of the group loudly says they can't accept him; one more person will sink the wing. Stephen listens carefully, and then lets himself slip into the sea. The gesture doesn't redeem him or alter what he has done, but it is a small contribution to the lives of others, as distinct from the large subtractions of lives he and his gang had been orchestrating before.

The gesture also takes us back to one of the film's truly magnificent shots. Stephen, speaking to John at a time when he is planning to have him killed, describes the conspirators — the gang he is not supposed to belong to — in what seems a deeply hypocritical way, presenting just the sort of condemnation he doesn't believe in. "They're fanatics," he says. "They combine a mad love of country with an equally mad indifference to life, their own as well as others'." But what we see on the screen, in the long gauzy close-up on Stephen's face as he speaks, is an awed admiration; he is describing his ideal, a dream of undiluted extremism. The speech ends, "They're cunning, unscrupulous, and . . . inspired."

The remarkable question, in the context of the war that has not yet come to America, is why Hitchcock should bother with moral and political complications of this kind. The movie ends with a brilliant pro-war splash. John Jones returns to England and makes the speech we have already heard part of, and the lights in the studio literally go out. "The Star-Spangled Banner" comes up on the sound track. Harry Hopkins, Franklin Delano Roosevelt's adviser and a strong supporter of American intervention in the war, sent Hitchcock a telegram, and Joseph Goebbels apparently admired the film as a piece of propaganda.

Are Stephen Fisher's politics and death part of this propaganda? Perhaps they are, but then what is the propaganda for? The erring humanity of the enemy is certainly not a tool much used in this department. But if the question is not whom we are fighting (or not yet fighting) against but what, then the enemy's mind is a good place to look. We need to know how that mind is different from ours, if it is, and if it isn't, how similar minds can reach such different conclusions. Hitchcock's refusal to demonize the Germans, or even the Nazis, is part of a view that thinks demonizing, even on behalf of democracy, is undemocratic. There are plenty of other reasons, of course, for a moviemaker to lend style to his villains; but for Hitchcock this was not a negligible one.

4

Enemies of the People

Not Yet

B Y THE TIME of Hitchcock's next war-related movie,
America had joined the fray — and as the film's title suggests, the fray had come to America. Hitchcock was able
to use history itself to dramatize its presence; he inserted into
Saboteur (1942) a documentary shot of the capsized French
liner the *Normandie*. The ship had docked in New York City
and been interned in 1939, just after the German invasion of Po-
land. In 1942, it caught fire and keeled over while it was being
converted into a troopship. Sabotage was widely suspected, although a congressional investigation concluded the fire was accidental. In the film we cut from the villainous saboteur in a
taxi to a shot of the half-sunken ship and then back to the man's
face: sly, contented, proud. Hitchcock says he got into all kinds
of trouble for suggesting the navy's security was so poor, but
poor security, we might say, was for Hitchcock a condition of
life and definitely a condition of film.

A man, Barry Kane, played by Robert Cummings, is wrongly
suspected of being a saboteur, and he rushes across America in
his quest to find the real enemy agent, a man "who doesn't mind
killing Americans for money." The chase ends up in New York
City, where the capsized ship is glimpsed, and the film closes on
the Statue of Liberty, from whose forehead the villain falls to
his death.

Two moments in the film are really memorable, the first

probably unintentionally, the second certainly as a reflection of Hitchcock's careful art. In New York Kane winds up at a high-society party where he runs into a sinister character he has already met on the road: Charles Tobin, a rich rancher, played by Otto Kruger with marvelous unction—Kruger made something of a specialty of such condescending roles. Kane had previously accused Tobin of being a fascist (not unreasonably since the man says he is "against voting"), and the man now speaks of "the moron millions" and "the competence of the totalitarian state," while the best Kane can do is go on about love being better than hatred. I don't think Kane is meant to be seen as losing these bouts, but he does. There is a magnificent shot of Tobin lounging at ease on a long sofa, arms stretched out along the back, portraits of two society ladies on the wall behind him. Is he going to stay around when the going gets tough? He says, "Havana will be very gay this season." With enemies like this one needs lots of friends, and something more than a few democratic slogans.

In the second memorable moment Kane is about to interrupt the same society event with an announcement about the presence of the Nazi sympathizers, and the camera scans the well-to-do crowd. These are Americans; this is New York, 1942 or thereabouts. These facts are not as consoling as they ought to be, and after a quick consultation of our fear on Kane's behalf, our worry about the reception he will get, we realize that we have been thinking he will meet with indifference or frivolity. These people are not Nazis, but they are not going to worry about Nazism either. Then as the camera lingers just a second too long on one of these portly figures, we realize Hitchcock is pursuing another thought. What if they are not indifferent? What if they are all Nazi sympathizers, a ballroom full of figures like the man with the missing piece of finger in *The 39 Steps*?

Hitchcock made *Shadow of a Doubt* in the middle of the war, between *Sabotage* and *Lifeboat*, and the war was certainly on his (and everyone else's) mind. The link between this film and the war lies in the sheer invisibility of the criminal aspect of Uncle Charlie to everyone except his niece and the cops. What Hitchcock's war looks like in his films is not so much a battlefield as a constantly invaded home front. The enemy is not just close; the enemy is within, in all the attitudes that failed to distinguish us from what we are fighting against. The immediate, haunting questions are whether we understand these attitudes and just what the difference is between what we might call local serial killing and the more professional national variety.

Hitchcock liked working with Thornton Wilder on *Shadow of a Doubt;* they were both interested in small towns — ours and theirs were the same. It was filmed and set in Santa Rosa, California, and Hitchcock took a lot of trouble in establishing the almost extravagant ordinariness of the place: public library, church, town square, policemen who know all the locals. The heroine's father and siblings are so ordinary, or so close to our expectations of the ordinary, that they're downright symbolic.

The film doesn't start in Santa Rosa, though. It starts in a place where a river, a run-down industrial landscape, and the Pulaski Skyway allow us to identify Newark, New Jersey. In a lodging house a man is lying on a bed, fully dressed in a pin-striped suit, quantities of cash scattered on the bedside table and on the floor. He doesn't look tired, but his tone when he speaks to the landlady is so bleakly polite as to sound suicidal. But it's probably not his own death that's on his mind. He's suspected of being the serial killer known as the Merry Widow murderer, and two detectives are waiting for him outside. The money, if he is the murderer, is a reminder of one widow's wealth, and his dark post-event mood suggests murder isn't fun. This man is simply identified as Uncle Charlie (played by Joseph Cotten).

In Santa Rosa his niece, "Charlie" Newton (Teresa Wright), is also lying on a bed and feeling gloomy, giving in to a teenage ennui that Hitchcock relates visually to the uncle's massive world-weariness. And when he comes to visit his family on the West Coast, we are strongly invited to think of these two persons together. They are both called Charlie, and the niece has fantasies about how close they are in temperament and ambition. But this is a closeness that hides a gulf of difference. Young Charlie has heard about her uncle's playboy past, but she's heard about it as romance and glamour, not murder. She tells him when they first talk that she knows all about him and that there is something "secret and wonderful" in his life. He rather grumpily says, "It's not good to find out too much, Charlie."

Uncle Charlie pretty much has to be the Merry Widow murderer, but the police also have another suspect in mind. The rule is this: A suspicion can be quite correct or quite wrong; either presumption can make a good story. And every suspicion, even a correct one, has a weak point, a chance of error. That is why it's only a suspicion.

In *Shadow of a Doubt,* we are watching the story of suspicion in reverse. Young Charlie does begin to find out too much, and her suspicion, tracked through news reports on the Merry Widow killings and Uncle Charlie's dubious behavior, becomes a belief. Even here, though, Hitchcock's devotion to uncertainty is exemplary.

Uncle Charlie repeatedly looms on the staircase of the family house like an expressionist villain—but is this a reason for thinking he's the killer? And most interesting of all, we hear on the sound track the strains of Franz Lehár's "Merry Widow Waltz," scored for too many trombones and not quite in tune, while a group of turn-of-the-century dancers in evening dress twirls around and around at a ball. We hear this tune and see this image during the opening credits, then when Uncle Charlie is worried about what others know, when the family is having dinner, and finally when young Charlie in the library puts two and two together about her uncle's crimes. This is a setup—a combination of image and sound — that no one in the film sees or hears, or even has in mind. The closest anyone gets is humming the tune or registering the verbal reference to the Merry Widow. No one except us, the audience, is treated to the orchestra and the period ball. I don't think Hitchcock uses an effect quite like this anywhere else in his films. It seems to say that the Merry Widow murderer is so unmistakably present that he drags a whole operetta into the movie with him. Or that young Charlie's suspicion is so powerful that it has the same result. But all the images and sounds say, strictly, is that the director has decided to give us a decorated illustration of what the newspapers are saying. Is it a real tip-off or just more rumor?

It's true that whatever lingering questions we may have about Uncle Charlie's guilt are laid to rest by his twice trying to murder his niece, once by loosening a step on the staircase she uses, once by locking her in a garage full of gas fumes. But then in a brilliant retake of the last scene of *Suspicion,* the two Charlies struggle on a train as it leaves the station, the door flung open. Obviously he is trying to kill her. This is his third attempt and this time he actually explains why: She knows too much. The struggle continues and then the uncle says, "Not yet, Charlie," as if the timing were up to her. More struggle and then the uncle says, "Now." At this point he is the one who falls from the train into the path of another one. Do we revise our view of the situation? He was certainly trying to kill young Charlie but perhaps he has changed his mind. Is he waiting until the train's speed picks up and he can throw himself out with a better chance of death? Probably not, but probability is only part of any story.

Young Charlie's suspicions of her uncle mean she won't help him or hide him, but her affection for him also means she won't turn him in to the police or do anything except try to persuade him to leave town. She knows he'll be arrested elsewhere, but at least the family won't have the press on its doorstep. As far as the town and the rest of the family are concerned, Uncle Charlie is a pure benefactor, a man who socializes, gives a talk to a ladies' club, puts his money in the local bank, makes donations to various charities. This is why the townsfolk are so sorry to see him leave, hope he'll return soon, and tell him, "We feel you're one of us."

Made of Iron

Hitchcock was always interested in who "we" are—he knew the pronoun could be a cover-up for all kinds of gangs, many of them convinced they were the best sort of people. And in his next war movie, *Lifeboat* (1944), he explored the idea of an American community. He said, speaking with unwonted earnestness, that it was "a microcosm of the war."

The movie opens with terrific economy, light means to large effects. We see not a ship but the smokestack of a ship. The credits come and go. The stack tilts, flames join the smoke coming from it, the stack topples into the water, sinks. All that is left is the sea, foaming, swirling, splashing, threatening to drown the camera. This sea is the real hero of the film. An American freighter carrying passengers has been torpedoed, and various survivors make it to the lifeboat. These people are indeed some sort of microcosm, a schematic picture of "America": fancy woman journalist, working-class guy with socialist leanings, fellow who loves to go dancing when he is at home, rich man who doesn't know how much he takes for granted, woman who's distressed about her affair with a married man, token African American, timid Canadian (who sounds English) just to remind us of the larger continent. The actors do what they can with these banalities. Tallulah Bankhead in particular is both funny and commanding, and Canada Lee brings real dignity to the black man's role even though he is charged with remembering Psalm 23 when everyone else has forgotten it, and trusting in heaven when all the others have lost whatever faith they had.

The movie's few moments of energy are concentrated in the German survivor who also makes it to the boat and everyone else's reaction to him. He is a wonderfully wily character who pretends not to speak English; he claims he is a crew member when he is actually a submarine captain who has a hidden compass to help him steer the boat in the wrong direction and a supply of water he chooses not to share with the parched and panicking others. He also kills a sick man because he is no longer of any use to anyone. A lovely fellow all round, full of smiles and songs, and extremely well played by Walter Slezak. In his confidence and calm this character is not unrelated to the Nazis in *Foreign Correspondent* and *Saboteur,* but Slezak is so unmistakably a fat, smiling bad guy that the movie's message is clear: All that liberal stuff about respecting the rights of others, even in wartime, has to be suspended in the case of the Germans — you just can't trust them. The argument is rammed home by the arrival at the end of a German survivor from another boat. He's just a kid, but he quickly pulls a gun on them and has to be disarmed. The film ends on his question: "Aren't you going to kill me?"

Why wouldn't they? They have just killed the submarine captain, when they finally awoke to the full scale of his deceptions. Several of them feel badly about this, because they know they became not a microcosm but a mob. But this legal and moral question doesn't alter the argument about never trusting Germans. Distrust them first and decide what to do with them afterward. This may be the only film in which Hitchcock pleads for a suspicion that is simply, amply justified. And a collective suspicion at that, where the bluntest, most chauvinist view of the enemy turns out to be right.

It is all the stranger therefore — this may well be the most interesting historical aspect of the film — that early reviews of *Lifeboat* saw it as a celebration of Nazi strength and willpower.

The *New York Times* film critic Bosley Crowther was worried by the fact that

> the most efficient and resourceful man in this "Lifeboat" is the Nazi, the man with "a plan." Nor is he an altogether repulsive or invidious type . . . [H]e is tricky and sometimes brutal, yes, but he is practical, ingenious and basically courageous in his lonely resolve. Some of his careful deceptions would be regarded as smart and heroic if they came from an American in the same spot.

Some, but what about the killing and the unremitting cold calculation? It is true that the survivors in the boat feel bereft when Slezak's character is gone; he was their "force," they say; they had taken him as their leader without knowing how far they had succumbed. Tallulah Bankhead had said, "He's made of iron, the rest of us are just flesh and blood." But since when did we want to be made of iron? The story looks momentarily like an allegory of the victory of Nazi principles in the wrong place, and Crowther seems to be endorsing just what he opposes. This thought is directly related to the idea that Bill Krohn, in his book *Hitchcock at Work,* attributes to Hitchcock and Ben Hecht as they started work on *Notorious* in 1944. They wanted to show, and even more so in 1946 when the film was released, that "the Nazis were not old hat." The Nazis are never old hat, and still less now perhaps. But the argument of the film — all of these war films — while supporting that broad intention, goes deeper. It says that you can think like a Nazi without being one. You can be one of them while imagining you are of us. All you have to do is overrate efficiency and strength, despise others, love purity, hate mixtures, and believe that ruthlessness and a sense of purpose are supreme virtues.

In late 1943 and early 1944 Hitchcock was in England, at the movie studios in Welwyn Garden City, shooting two three-reeler films. The production company was called, appropriately enough, Phoenix Londres, an enterprise sponsored by the Ministry of Information and devoted to the rescue of France from the ashes of defeat. The films were in French, spoken mainly by French actors, translated from English scripts written in English (by Angus MacPhail and J.O.C. Orton). One translation effect is particularly evocative in a Hitchcock context. In *Bon Voyage* the commanding officer of the Free French group is debriefing the Scottish airman who has escaped from occupied France, and who asks the officer how he knows so much about what is going on across the Channel. He says he is very intelligent, meaning he has good intelligence, but of course Hitchcock wouldn't really want to distinguish between the meanings anyway. Having intelligence in both senses is a tricky question: It's about what you know and about what you can do with what you know.

Bon Voyage recounts this airman's escape and his review of it with the French officer in England. The French officer keeps offering corrections to the airman's account, and we see those in a kind of hypothetical flashback, the way the airman would have seen things if he had known differently. It turns out that the person who helped him escape to England was a Polish collaborator serving as a German agent. His task was to infiltrate the Resistance, and his (genuine) aid to the Scotsman was a bluff to put the French off guard. As with his earlier killing of another German agent: anything to establish credentials. The truth too can serve in a world of lies, and more effectively than a feeble untruth anytime.

Bon Voyage, for all the interest of the double deception, is a little clumsy as a film; *Aventure Malgache* is more delicate and complicated. A group of French actors is preparing to go onstage in a play in London. One of them, Paul Clarus, a former lawyer in Madagascar, decides to help another actor with his part by telling him a story about a villain he knew, a certain Jean Michel, who resembles the character his companion is playing. Clarus was organizing resistance on the island; Michel was the Vichy regime's chief of police. Clarus describes in detail, and the film shows, Michel's dogged and angry hounding of the opposition, his prying of information out of subordinates, his particular animus against Clarus. He says at one point that he wants proof at any price: *"Je veux des épreuves à tout prix."* This may not seem an unreasonable thing to want, but in a Hitchcock film it's a clear sign of a person dedicated to error. Michel does get some incriminating evidence — Clarus is betrayed by a colleague who talked too much to his mistress — and he has Clarus sent to a penal colony. Or not quite, since the boat taking him there is intercepted by a British warship and Clarus escapes to England.

Hitchcock, although keen to support the Resistance, didn't underestimate its enemies. This wasn't at all the message anyone wanted, and the film was never released. By the end of the story the actor playing the man who resembles Michel has so thoroughly absorbed himself in the role that he accuses Clarus of attacking him. Is this a joke on the actor's part, or has he really been carried away into total identification? The man murmurs, "Only rehearsing," but is this true? Hitchcock is not going to tell us, and of course the question is itself part of the atmosphere he has created, part of his suggestion that truth and lies are uncertain war zones. As the film ends, the actors leave the dressing room and the play starts.

Hitchcock was also listed as "treatment advisor" on a film called *Memory of the Camps.* It was made up of footage shot by British, American, and Russian cameramen in the last days of the European war and just after it. The Germans surrendered in May 1945, and Hitchcock was in London discussing the photography in June. He was very keen to recommend wide shots establishing locality, so that historical or geographical elements could not be taken out or put in during editing. The master of montage knew what montage could do to the raw truth.

The raw truth was almost unbearable. Half the film as we have it centers on the concentration camp at Bergen-Belsen, although seven other camps are also named and described: Dachau, Buchenwald, Ebensee, Mauthausen, Ohrdruf, Wöbbelin, Auschwitz. In most cases numbers of the dead are given: 30,000 here, 32,000 there, 55,000 here, 4 million there. The commentary tells us that the camps contained "nothing but filth and death," and the frames show very little else except a great deal of bone. Many of these people must have looked just like skeletons when they were still alive. The frames show piles of emaciated corpses, or corpses being dropped one by one into a vast common grave. Some of the images are beautifully composed: sunlight falling sharp on a grave, soldiers and other bystanders casting shadows along the edge. One shot of corpses stacked like items in a warehouse recalls a medieval frieze, a dance worse than death, as many images in Alain Resnais's *Night and Fog* also do. Local German mayors and other civil leaders were brought to watch these burials, and the commentary contains so much emphasis on the idea that the Germans cannot *not* have known about the camps and what happened in them that it is hard to see how the film could ever have served its supposed purpose: to cheer the Germans up and help them get on with reconstruction. But then it's very hard to see what sort of Allied film would help with this aim, and whatever the original intention this is not a film for the defeated country — or not for that country in particular.

The commentary, written in 1945 by Richard Crossman and Colin Wills, and spoken by Trevor Howard in the version released much later, is rather tired in tone, as if worn out by horror, occasionally sarcastic ("The S.S. men are not so spick and span now"), but ultimately thoughtful rather than accusatory. Its last words are "But, by God's grace, we who live will learn."

The film's narrative shape uses a historical irony to set the grim visual in context. It starts with footage of crowds massing to see Hitler, the führer offering his quick mechanical salute with half an arm, then swiftly traces the fortunes of the war before cutting to rural Germany, all orchards, farms, and rustic peace. Finally we arrive at Bergen-Belsen. The sequence invites us to track two versions of the same question: How could these people have followed this man with such virulent enthusiasm, and how could this quiet place have provided a setting for so much forced dying?

The commentary uses a phrase that seems a little strange in context, and that gets stranger still when we see it picked up by Jean-Luc Godard in his film *Histoire(s) du cinéma*. The Germans, we are told in *Memory of the Camps*, were hoping to arrive, through Hitler and the Nazis, at "a place in the sun at last." Godard's extravagant phrase, delivered in voice-over, is "And if George Stevens hadn't been the first to use the first sixteen-millimeter color film at Auschwitz and Ravensbrück, there's no doubt that Elizabeth Taylor's happiness would never have found a place in the sun." The French philosopher Jacques Rancière, in his book *The Future of the Image*, glosses this weird connection as meaning that "[Taylor] has positively merited this happiness because George Stevens has positively filmed the camps and thus performed the task of the cinematic sentence-image." That is, Stevens's documentary conscience excuses the unbroken American dream, allows him to make *A Place in the Sun.* Surely this reading misses too much, and above all fails to honor Godard's deliberate avoidance of pedestrian logic.

The Germans wanted a place in the sun and became mass murderers because there were too many people in the way, or complicating their idea of the way. The Americans wanted and still want a place in the sun, and photographed the camps and sentimental films with the same color film — this is part of the history of cinema. What I see in the use of the phrase "a place in the sun" in these two very different films is an ambivalence about national aspirations — do we all want a place in the sun or is it easy to sneer at the idea? — and a question about film. Is it our judge or our accomplice? Could it be both? It's not true in any sense that Stevens's documentary work at the end of the war allowed him to make Hollywood movies. It is true that the same technology can live very different lives.

Memory of the Camps is not a Hitchcock work. But his association with the film is important, and not only because of what it says about his relation to the war and its aftermath. For me the most memorable shot in the film — and I was intrigued to discover that the film critic Richard Brody, in a piece in the January 9, 2014 edition of the *New Yorker* titled "Hitchcock and the Holocaust," had picked out the same image — is not one of corpses or graves or bones, memorable as those shots are. It is the sight of the burning huts at Bergen-Belsen. They are being burned for health reasons, because typhus is spreading among the prisoners left alive, but there is something about the consuming flames, their violent, unruly energy, their promise of complete erasure, that puts them in another field of meaning.

Brody writes: "The flames . . . have a metaphorical power — suggesting both the incineration of millions of corpses, and a sort of divine vengeance against the perpetrators — that raises the images outside the realm of journalism and into a terrifying realm of art." There's no suggestion of vengeance for me, since I'm inclined to see the flames as colluding with the perpetrators, eerily, horribly continuing their work in our imagination. But the principle of metaphorical power remains the same, and I'm sure I would not have felt any of this if I hadn't known of Hitchcock's involvement in the film. I don't attribute the shot to his guidance; I am not making a rational or causal claim. Indeed, this particular sequence was probably completed before Hitchcock came to work on the film. But Hitchcock can change the way we see. Sometimes the name alone will effect the change, and our minds do the rest. The graves and the bones are almost too solid for Hitchcock's world. The flames are a reminder that traces of human life can vanish like the lady in a movie, and without traces we have no history.

The Next Time

In *Spellbound* Hitchcock's great coup was recruiting Ingrid Bergman: alert, inventive, always present, and infinitely loved by the camera. Especially by Hitchcock's. He had less luck with Salvador Dalí and with Gregory Peck: The first was too eccentric for the producer, David Selznick, and the second too decently wooden for his creepy role. In *Notorious,* with Cary Grant's help, Bergman came into her own, bringing with her a history that was part of her plot as well as the movie's.

She plays Alicia, a young woman whose father is tried for and convicted of treason against the United States. The time is April 1946; the place is Miami. A door opens to let us into the courtroom, and we see the accused from behind — that's all we see of him. Asked if he has anything to say for himself he starts an unrepentant diatribe about what will happen "the next time," and his lawyer quiets him down. The judge passes sentence: twenty years. Outside the courtroom, a crowd of newsmen with flashing cameras is waiting for Alicia, pressing her for responses to her father's conviction. Two other men are waiting there too: FBI agents, with their eye on a possible new recruit.

The next shot places us in Alicia's house, where a party is taking place and she is more than a little tipsy. We catch sight of another man only from the back. We see no more of him till the other guests leave. When the camera tracks around him we see he is Cary Grant, but we don't know what he is doing at the party. Or why he agrees to go for a drive with the now quite drunk Alicia at the wheel. He is a calm enough passenger to annoy her and provoke her to faster speeds — "I don't like gentlemen who grin at me," she says. Everything becomes clear when a cop pulls Alicia over. He is about to give her a ticket, but Grant hands over his ID. The cop salutes respectfully and leaves them to it. Even Alicia gets it now: He's an FBI agent spying on her. She doesn't take kindly to this, and he has to knock her out with a punch to take her home.

Actually he's not spying on her — the FBI has been doing that for a while, and its records show Alicia's disagreements with her father about his allegiances, which is why it thinks she may be willing to work for the bureau. The agent, Devlin, is out to recruit her for a job in Rio de Janeiro infiltrating a Nazi network — a branch, we later learn, "of the combine that built up the German war machine and hopes to keep on going." (Grant's charm has to work quite hard against some of the lines he is given.) Devlin says, "I've got a job for you . . . And you could make up a little for your daddy's peculiarities." She asks why she should, and he says patriotism. She says the word gives her a pain and adds a couple of cruel, if accurate, definitions of what patriotism can mean in practice. But then Devlin plays a record of a conversation with her father in which she says, "I love this country, do you understand that?" Ah yes, that sort of patriot. She takes the job.

In Rio, Alicia and Devlin spend some time together before the details of her job come through. They fall in love, she openly and vulnerably, he rather guardedly. There is an element of history here, or rather the chance of an escape from one history into another. Alicia loves Devlin, but she loves even more the chance of a fresh start, a changed life, a departure from the drinking and love affairs of her recent years. What sort of chance is this? Devlin doesn't know whether he can trust her ability to change, but above all is caught between two other, less attractive sources of suspicion: his job and his fear of attractive women. When he is told of Alicia's mission — to pick up her relationship with a former suitor of hers, a friend of her father's, who is part of the combine — he is shocked and would like to keep her out of it, drawing his superiors' ire and impatience for trying to do so. But when he sees her again he says nothing of this, allows her to believe he did not protest at all, that he doesn't care (enough) about whom she has to hang out with or what she has to do. This scene is excruciating and brilliantly played by both actors: Grant awkward, even mildly angry, rather than affectionate; Bergman desolate although capable of brittle jokes — of course she thinks his attitude has to do solely with his failure to believe in her, in her capacity to turn history around.

A little later Hitchcock finds an extraordinary cinematic image for this tribulation. Alicia gets together with her former suitor, Alex Sebastian, and at one point she and Devlin have to fake a kiss so it will look as if they are engaged in a romance, thus avoiding detection as they conspire to steal the key to Sebastian's wine cellars, where the combine's precious uranium ore is kept. They have to imitate, that is, what used to be the case, and what is still the case beneath their current professional performance and the anxious distrust each now has of the other's feelings. We can't *not* remember the tender, lingering kisses we have seen them exchange before, and we can't, now, believe this kiss is not the real thing as we look at it. Even Sebastian, the man who is supposed to be taken in, knows it is the real thing. Devlin and Alicia must feel this too, even if they don't know for certain it is the case — much suspicion remains to be conquered on his part, much despair to be lived through on hers. This piece of deception in which no one is deceived is pure Hitchcock, one of his most memorable salutes to the insidious empire of appearances. Even when they are true they are still an act. Or only a touch of fakery will make them true.

Sebastian is played by Claude Rains with such grace and kindness we not only forget he is a Nazi, but we don't see how he could be one. When he goes to his death at the end of the movie, doomed by his colleagues for his relationship with Alicia and the information she has passed on to the FBI, we can't help but mourn for him — even if he had been slowly poisoning Alicia, and she had been near death. Well, maybe we don't mourn, but something like pity floats briefly up as he returns to his house and execution. He was too likable, too gracious not to be missed. And he did love Alicia, even if he was killing her.

There is another reason to be sorry for him: his august mother. Claude Rains was English, naturalized American in 1939; but we may think of him as French because of his role in *Casablanca*. However, there is nothing in *Notorious* to indicate his nationality except for his character's mother, magnificently played by Leopoldine Konstantin as an adamant parody of a Prussian tyrant — she was born in Moravia, then part of the Austro-Hungarian Empire — and a reminder that the Nazis were just hoodlums compared with the Allies' classier enemies. Seeing him caught between this terrifying lady and Ingrid Bergman's Alicia, we can only admire him for daring to be interested in Alicia. Konstantin wasn't a Nazi or a Prussian, just a very good actress who knew how to create a monster (her word for this part) when she was asked to.

The film ends with a door closing on Sebastian as he goes in to his death. There is no final embrace between Alicia and Devlin, no assurance even that she will survive the poison that has so weakened her. We can imagine this if we like, and most of us do. What we must imagine, I think, is that she now believes he loves her, and so is able to believe in herself, and that he is no longer afraid of her backsliding into drink and looseness of life. To fill out the picture we need to remember Alicia's earlier words when she is told her father has killed himself in prison — with poison, foreshadowing her own poisoning. "I remember

how nice he once was..." she says. "Very nice." And then, ex-
plaining her odd sense of liberation, "You see, I don't have to
hate him anymore. Or myself." We might adopt Godard's non-
logic here to spell out the implication: If Alicia and Devlin had
not together overcome her history and his fear, the Nazis would
have been on the way to winning, and not only in the movies.

5

Changing Light

The New World

I N *HITCHCOCK AT WORK,* Bill Krohn tells us that on the first day of shooting *Strangers on a Train* Hitchcock "announced to cast and crew that none of his previous pictures counted — today was the real beginning of his film-making career." This was some sixteen years before he told Truffaut that "*The Lodger* was the first true 'Hitchcock movie.'" He also said on another occasion, "I think you'll find that the real start of my career was *The Man Who Knew Too Much*" — referring to the first movie of that name. He was entitled to change his mind, of course, but he could have been right each time. He could have made his first "true" movie at one moment and started his career at another. He could have started his American career with a film that picked up, made clear, and concentrated what he had been trying to do since he settled in his new country. He was four years away from becoming an American citizen.

What he was mainly trying to do, it seems, was make American films in America, as distinct from English ones, and to carry some of the energies and preoccupations of his wartime films into the years of peace. *The Paradine Case* (1947) and *Stage Fright* (1950) were commissions that offered no real advance in either direction, and *Under Capricorn,* in Hitchcock's view, was an error he made just for the sake of signing up Ingrid Bergman. *Rope* (1948) was something different, however: a complex technical experiment in which echoes of Nazi theories took on a new philosophical life.

In *Shadow of a Doubt,* we already heard Uncle Charlie in the mode of the amateur fascist, spouting to his niece all kinds of pseudo-Nietzschean rubbish about who is fit to live and who isn't. "The whole world's a joke to me," he says, but "the silly wives" of rich men are the people who chiefly attract his scornful attention: "these useless women . . . smelling of money, proud of their jewelry but of nothing else." When young Charlie protests that they are human, her uncle says, "Are they human, or are they fat, wheezing animals, hmm?" They could be that and human too, but Uncle Charlie's contempt doesn't need precision. And it's not as if he's murdering them on principle, cleaning up the bejeweled sties of the wealthy. Or is he? What is all this talk about? I suppose we are to take it as the superficial, displaced language of a need to kill that has other grounds, even if the money is never going to be entirely irrelevant.

In *Rope,* Uncle Charlie's displaced argument becomes the articulated motive, and what is most interesting about the film's development is that its weakest dramatic moments concern the failure to argue the human case against murder. In fact, the film doesn't really have strong dramatic moments because its subject is a situation rather than a story — its effect on us is rather like that of walking around an installation. This partly has to do with Hitchcock's experiment. He famously shot the whole film in takes lasting from four to ten minutes and disguised the breaks so that it seems as if the film passes without a single cut. But it has even more to do with the structure Hitchcock borrowed from Patrick Hamilton's play, which in turn was based on a notorious historical case. Nathan Leopold and Richard Loeb were two rich young men who murdered a child to prove they could do it. In Hitchcock's film the young men are college students who murder one of their friends, purportedly carrying out the theories of their schoolteacher, but no doubt following other, less dutiful impulses as well. "We killed for the sake of danger," one of the men says, "and for the sake of killing. We're alive." Later he speaks of their "angle" as "the artistic one."

The film opens with a shot of a New York City street, cars passing, children crossing. We see an apartment with long windows whose curtains are all drawn. We hear a gasp, and the camera takes us behind the curtains into a room. Two young men, Brandon and Phillip, played by John Dall and Farley Granger, have just finished strangling a third man — or Phillip has completed the strangling with Brandon's insistent encouragement and close cooperation. Phillip looks wasted by the effort, and Brandon ecstatic. Critics have spoken of a post-orgasm effect here, and they are almost certainly heeding just the cue Hitchcock wanted them to heed. "I felt tremendously exhilarated," Brandon says later, putting it mildly. This is the last moment of real excitement in the film, though; it's all situational from here on.

Brandon and Phillip put the body in a long chest and it stays there throughout the film. A buffet dinner is served on the chest rather than the dining-room table, since Brandon thinks the secret presence of their victim will give spice to the evening, but of course the only savorer of the spice is Brandon himself. The guests are the victim's parents and fiancée, as well as another schoolmate who is the fiancée's ex-boyfriend and the teacher who is notionally responsible for all this, a man called Rupert, played by a suave and plausibly sinister James Stewart: nothing like a manifestly nice man for an effective villain. Rupert is said to have taught that "murder is a crime for most men, but a privilege for the few." But he's not the villain, the film finally suggests, just a man who plays with dangerous ideas.

Within the film Rupert gets a whole scene to expound his theory of the right of superior people to kill their manifest inferiors. "Think of the problems it would solve," he says, adding that "murder is, or should be, an art — not one of the 'seven lively,' perhaps, but..." He's not persuasive, but he is darkly funny. The dead boy's father protests; he doesn't like this kind of talk at all. At the end of the movie, when Rupert has figured out what Brandon and Phillip have done and is ready to turn them in — we hear the sound of police sirens getting nearer — Rupert himself starts talking like a good old humanist, firm respecter of the right of even the least deserving of humans to have their day. "You've given my words a meaning I never dreamed of," he says to Brandon, but he's deluding himself. Brandon didn't give the words a different meaning; he just put the meaning into practice.

And the entire time the body sits there. We know this and so do the murderers, but no one else does until the very end. It is the one thing we know, the only thing we can think about, and there are camera angles on the chest that make our knowledge almost unbearable, a secret we wish we had not been shown. It's not that we fear the body will be discovered, the killers exposed. We might feel this had not the two men each in his way made this sympathy impossible, Phillip because he twitches and panics throughout and Brandon because he is magisterially enjoying what he takes to be his triumph and his joke. What we feel, I think, is that it would be too awful if the parents or the fiancée knew what we know. The physical proximity of the body acts as a kind of figure for the thinness of the membrane, the screen of chance, that separates us all from violence and demise. Even in Arcadia, death says it is in the old legends; even in well-heeled Manhattan, death says it's now just under the table.

If Rupert is not persuasive in his superman theory and Brandon even less persuasive about his right to put that theory into practice — "He and I," he says of Phillip and himself, "have lived out what you and I have talked" — how can the argument against them be less persuasive still? I think this is a variant on

Hitchcock's insistence on the smoothness of the Nazis and the complacency of the English before the war. He is suggesting that the respect for life is partial and intermittent among us, that too many of us don't care about it or pretend we don't care, and that caring itself is not enough anyway. Where talk turns into dangerous action, we need to act, not just talk back belatedly, spluttering away on the moral high ground. Tales of murder, in such a context, are a dark amusement, difficult forms of a question we may not be able to answer. To go from *Rope* to *Strangers on a Train,* as Hitchcock did in three years, is a huge step artistically, from interesting practice to accomplished performance; but intellectually it is only a small hop.

So Long at the Fair

The Hitchcock of *Strangers on a Train* doesn't go in for Welles's very low camera angles, converting his characters into looming giants. But he rarely places his shots at eye level; there is quite a bit of looming, even if there are no giants, and sometimes the frame is tilted sideways. In one take, when Bruno Anthony (Robert Walker) is about to murder a woman, the combination of a low angle and a fish-eye lens makes his arms and hands look like the encroaching pincers of some horror-movie insect. There are iron gates that create the effect of prison bars, and there are familiar Washington monuments that seem as if they couldn't exist anywhere except in a movie or on a postcard.

Bill Krohn notes astutely that "Bruno, filmed against Washington backdrops, reflects Cold War paranoia about homosexual spies blackmailing 'susceptible' government employees into selling government secrets," but there is also a simpler, broader reading of these images. This is "Washington," and by extension America, pictured as slightly unreal and yet really vulnerable, not only because its secrets are at risk, but because even without the Cold War it could always be drastically unsettled by the unruly effects of its own wishes or even half-wishes. There are two remarkable shots of Bruno standing on the steps of the Jefferson Memorial, a tiny, smartly dressed figure against the vast white pillars. He's not doing anything except standing, and nothing in the plot leads to or from his presence at this place. He is literally there within the story, I assume, in the sense that he is not supposed to be a fantasy. But he functions as a fantasy because otherwise the shots don't mean anything. Guy Haines (Farley Granger) sees the small speck on the monument from a distance as he walks past and then again as a taxi takes him back along the route. The speck is what threatens his ambition, which is to quit the world of tennis in which he is a well-known star and go into politics, and his ambition is solidified into the monument. His inability either to ignore or deal with the speck is what is messing up his life. And by extension, these stark, brilliant, narratively irrelevant shots are saying that a similar inability may haunt the official America the monument represents. Donald Spoto writes of the figure of Bruno as "a malignant stain . . . a blot on the order of things," which nicely catches the feeling of the scene but exports the problem from America to the universe.

Hitchcock also uses the name of an actual place for symbolic effect in the setting of his murder scene. This is Metcalf, the town mentioned in the Patricia Highsmith novel on which the movie is based. But her Metcalf is in Texas and presumably has whatever it takes to make a town. Hitchcock's Metcalf is somewhere between Forest Hills in Queens, New York, and Washington, DC, between tennis and politics, and consists, as far as we can see, only of a railway station, a suburban street, a record shop, and a fairground. The railway station is where Guy gets off the train when he goes to visit his wife, Miriam (and where Hitchcock makes a cameo appearance boarding a train with a double bass as his luggage), the record shop is where Guy and Miriam quarrel, the street is where she lives, and the fairground is where she dies. Very economical; all you need a town to be. Visits, marriage, life, death.

The plot of *Strangers on a Train* is well known. Two men, one a top-rank tennis player and the other a spoiled, misbehaving son of a rich man, meet when they sit opposite each other. Bruno knows all about Guy, including his relationship with his unfaithful wife (who is about to refuse to agree to a divorce) and his romance with a senator's daughter, and comes up with an ingenious scheme. Since the real objection to murder is not moral but prudential — we are afraid of getting caught — and since the reason murderers are caught is because they have motives, all we need to do is to swap murders, and the possibility of being traced evaporates. Crisscross, as Bruno says. So Bruno could do Guy's murder and take out the hindering wife, and Guy could do Bruno's, getting rid of the hated father. Guy says, with some reason, "What do you mean, my murder?," and patronizingly pretends to admire his scheme. He leaves the train at Metcalf, convinced Bruno is crazy. His failure to object is often taken as a sign of his collusion, but it's worth remembering that even his strenuous opposition to the plan would have worked in just the same way. Bruno doesn't need consent, and if he did he could read denial or any form of response at all as permission to continue.

Bruno does the murder, and the rest of the movie involves his waiting for Guy to complete his (unaccepted) part of the deal. Why doesn't Guy just go to the police? The standard answer to this question is that he feels guilty because he has wanted the crime committed even if he didn't do it. A better answer is the more Hitchcockian one: He doesn't go to the police because he is afraid of them and doesn't think they will believe his story. He is probably right. He behaves like a guilty person not because he is guilty, but because that is how a lot of us behave when we think about the police. He had certainly struggled violently with Miriam in the record shop when they quarreled, and he had told his current girlfriend that he wanted to strangle his wife. But the tempting theory that figures of speech are buried wishes, the indirect naming of what we would like to do directly, is only a piece of the subtle truth this movie is after. Guy wants Miriam out of the way but he doesn't necessarily want her dead, even if he says he does, and the theory about figures of speech is Bruno's and not the movie's own — as it might well have been in an earlier Hitchcock film. People die rather casually in Hitchcock's English works; the moral question is either intimated or internalized. In his American films people mostly die circumstantially and at length, as if to remind us of the finality of the event, and indeed to point out the difference between the wish to be rid of someone and the desire for his or her death.

When Bruno kills Miriam in the fairground, the camera lingers over all kinds of effects apart from that of the looming insect. His lighter (Guy's lighter, actually, left in the train and picked up by Bruno) allows an eerie gleam to play on Miriam's face; her glasses fall to the ground and the whole of the slow strangling is reflected in one of the lenses, as if in a funhouse mirror. We don't, I assume, give any real consideration at this point to Bruno's state of mind; we just take him for the disassociated psychopath he appears to be. But later, at a party in the senator's house, when he starts to illustrate his theory of everyone wanting to murder someone, he grasps a lady by the throat and loses control of the game he thinks he is playing, and we have to think differently about him. He looks across the room at the senator's younger daughter (played by Pat Hitchcock, in her largest role in one of her father's films). Hitchcock has already established the fact that this girl reminds Bruno of Miriam, mainly because she too wears glasses, but what we didn't know until now is that Bruno is disturbed by his own role as murderer. The resemblance triggers a shock in him, and he goes into a form of trance, gripping the lady's neck without any consciousness of what he is now doing, but fully possessed by the memory of what he once did. The music of the fairground rises in the sound track, the threatened lady shrieks, and Bruno passes out just in time not to have killed her.

So even Bruno, who believes that one should do "everything" in life, that every dream should be translated into reality if at all possible, hasn't shifted from theory to practice without grave consequences; and the larger point concerning Guy and Miriam is more elusive but also, I think, more frightening than the straightforward psychological reading of what Guy secretly or overtly wishes. Psychology in Hitchcock is often shallow rather than deep, and compelling for that reason: close to the action, not hidden from sight, a matter not of interpretation but of emergency response. How might we cope, for example, if reality conspired for us rather than against us? Hitchcock invites us not to beware of what we wish for, or to think of casual slogans as Freudian slips, but to watch out for those moments when chance itself, without any serious invitation on our part, converts our rage and frustration into action we can't revoke. As if we had an agent, an unbidden crony like Bruno, who takes care of what he thinks we want. Does he know what we want? No, but he doesn't care — chance *can't* care. The implication is not that anyone can do anything but that anything can happen to anyone, the presumption of an erratic but extensive contingency.

A long tradition of great novels and movies invites us to believe there is only one form of narrative logic: What happens in the written or pictured world is what would probably happen in "reality." We know better than this — we couldn't much enjoy a novel or a movie if we didn't — but we are not in the habit of thinking of other working logics. *Strangers on a Train,* like the rather different *Who Framed Roger Rabbit* (1988), is among other things a textbook introduction to these alternatives.

Things happen in *Roger Rabbit*, for example, not when they plausibly might but when they get the best laugh, and characters behave the way they do because they are "drawn like that." We have already seen Bruno standing on the steps of the Jefferson Memorial. Why is he there? Because it's scary (for us and Guy) to see him there; because he is everywhere; because Hitchcock is not averse to symbolism. None of these reasons has anything to do with the movie's action.

The most extravagant departure from the necessities of real-world logic occurs at the end of the movie, but here we are looking at something like a small, brilliant film in its own right. Narratives have needs, often quite compatible with plausible behavior, sometimes not, and sometimes crying out for a flamboyant response. Hitchcock's needs at the end of *Strangers on a Train* are quite complicated but could be met in many ways. Hitchcock didn't have to set his murder in a fairground, or turn his closing scene into a small apocalypse. All he needed to do was have Bruno kill Miriam somewhere (anywhere) and have him narrowly thwarted at the end in his scheme to plant Guy's lighter at the scene of the crime. Narrowly in order to create suspense and excitement; and thwarted because Bruno can't get away with murder — that would mean his theory of exchange was correct, even if the practice was only half complete.

If we compare these modest requirements with what we see on-screen we begin to have an idea of what moviemaking looks like: an opportunity to let the baroque energies of your imagination have a day out. Before Bruno can plant the lighter on the fairground island where he killed Miriam, Guy catches up with him and both board a merry-go-round. A policeman aiming presumably at Guy, who is still the chief official suspect, shoots the ride operator, who dies instantly, dragging down a handle that accelerates the rotation of the machine. The ride turns faster and faster, the music speeds up. Bruno and Guy slug it out as if they were in an old western saloon. Several of the children on the rising and falling horses are delighted with the new pace, others are terrified. Off the merry-go-round, mothers are scared for their offspring, the police are helpless, and a brave, toothless old man says he knows how to stop the machine — by crawling underneath the whirling ride. Hitchcock said he continued long after to have nightmares about this man, "since this was actually as dangerous as it appeared to be and if he had raised his head just an inch or two he would certainly have been killed." The poor fellow takes what feels like half an hour to get to the center and bring the machine to a halt. Meanwhile a small child almost falls off the merry-go-round but is saved by Guy, who takes time out from his fight with Bruno to effect this rescue. This is probably a bit of visual sarcasm from Hitchcock. It says, "I thought you'd like to be reminded that the good guy is the good guy," or "You do believe in good guys, don't you?" Halting the machine, however, turns out not to be the quiet solution we were hoping for. The speed of the thing is such that stopping means crashing. The whole merry-go-round crumbles, fatally crushing Bruno in the process. We don't get a chance to count the other victims, but the sense of something monstrous and unintended filling the screen is unmistakable. The dying Bruno is unrepentant and still keen on incriminating Guy. But then his hand opens to reveal the lighter, and the story finally becomes clear even to the police.

We don't need to interpret this scene — or if you prefer, we can pile up all the interpretations we fancy — only to recognize what we have already seen: a fast, noisy movie evocation of amusement, speed, danger, confusion, machinery, and damage. Or to put that another way: a meticulously controlled picture of an out-of-control situation. Any awareness we may have of this scene's careful construction plays beautifully against what it shows. We might think again of Hitchcock's dislike of disorder and conclude that only a very intense form of this dislike would provoke such a painstaking show of its object. I would add too that we are looking not only at Hitchcock's psyche but at his take on the anxieties of America, that place where guns are apt to kill the wrong people and machinery, literal and metaphorical, is very often taken for granted until it crashes.

Dizzy Money

After *Strangers on a Train* Hitchcock made three more films for Warner Bros. (*I Confess, Dial M for Murder, The Wrong Man*), and then a series of films for Paramount (*Rear Window, To Catch a Thief, The Trouble with Harry, The Man Who Knew Too Much,* and *Vertigo*). He found his way to this studio as a director on loan from Warner, to whom he was under contract, but soon signed a new deal with Paramount itself, and the period of what McGilligan calls "dizzy money" began. Hitchcock's agent by this point was Lew Wasserman, who put this profitable arrangement together — and later helped him and Alma to become part owners of Universal Studios. After the five films for Paramount (six if we include *Psycho,* which was a Paramount coproduction) and one for MGM, he stayed with Universal for the rest of his career. Wasserman also suggested Hitchcock's involvement in television, resulting in his two series, first *Alfred Hitchcock Presents* and then *The Alfred Hitchcock Hour,* which, as David Thomson says, "changed him more than he could have guessed." This is true in all kinds of interesting ways. Hitchcock became famous again, or more famous, or famous differently; and yet this Hitchcock was not entirely the old one. It is worth remembering, as John Russell Taylor wrote, "how revolutionary it was, back in those relatively early days of television, for a front-rank, top-class movie director to involve himself in any way with this trashy, despised medium."

Much has been written about the "Hitchcock blonde," as if all the blond women in his films were the same, or as if he had invented the idea of the seductive dame with fair hair. In fact, Hitchcock, like everyone else after Anita Loos, knew that gentlemen preferred blondes, and that fellows who were not gentlemen preferred them possibly even more. That's what those flashing mentions of curls are about in *The Lodger,* and that's what the elaborate hairdos of Kim Novak and Tippi Hedren are about in *Vertigo* and *The Birds.* Hitchcock told Truffaut that blondes were thought to be more "sophisticated" than brunettes, therefore harder to suspect, and therefore all the more shocking as spectacles when they came apart or turned out to be whores. This was probably never true as a general proposition, and in any case by the time Hitchcock said it our expectations were pretty much the opposite. As early as *Blackmail* we feel the blond heroine, played by Anny Ondra, is a tease because she is a blonde, not in spite of the fact.

Apart from these tired tropes, there is really only one Hitchcock blonde: Grace Kelly as she appears in *Dial M for Murder, Rear Window,* and especially *To Catch a Thief.* The projected figure here is not the sophisticated lady with fire in her loins, but the icy girl who turns out to be lots of fun. Forget about the innuendo that runs through the last of those movies and the Kelly character's perfect control of all the sexual action that occurs. Just listen to her tell Cary Grant at the end that they will be very happy together, and how much she likes his house. Oh yes, and how much "Mother will love it up here." Her relish in the joke suggests that primness itself can be a mode of seduction and aggravation.

Hitchcock tried to re-create this figure with Eva Marie Saint in *North by Northwest* with some success. She couldn't quite convey the mystery and the fun behind the poise, but she had style and she had irony. With Kim Novak in *Vertigo* he didn't even try. She is wonderfully effective in this movie but she is not a Hitchcock blonde, because she suggests no mischief, has no Kelly-style second personality behind the earnest image. There is nothing behind the rather static beauty, because as a blonde she is a fiction within the fiction, a man's idea of woman as a statue. With Tippi Hedren in *The Birds* and *Marnie*, Hitchcock did try again, but with different and personally damaging results. Hedren *looks* like a reincarnation of Grace Kelly, perhaps more the creation of Edith Head, the designer, than of Hitchcock. Or of the hairstylists Virginia Darcy and Alexandre of Paris. But then what her character finally suggests is not a calm beauty that conceals interesting energies, but an artful confection waiting to be destroyed — a horrible combination of Hedren's limitations as an actress and Hitchcock's crossing a line into what used to be a world only of his imagination.

Did Hitchcock just look at the women he admired? Was he in love with Grace Kelly or Ingrid Bergman? He certainly crossed a line with Tippi Hedren, and almost certainly made passes at other actresses. So was his repeated claim to be impotent a lie, or did he just make the passes impotent men can make? David Freeman, who worked with Hitchcock on his last, uncompleted film, didn't know about the impotence claim and was surprised to hear Hitchcock say, "Alma and I do not have relations. Haven't for years." Freeman comments:

> I almost blush now to admit it, but I thought the man was talking about relatives ... Whether the remark about his marriage was true or not, only the principals could say for sure. But it's clear that's what he wanted the record to say. To say to the world that sex and passion, the absolute fundament of his work, was not a part of his marriage, was surely to be trying to say: "I am my films, my films are me. If you want to know either, look at them, my spiritual legacy, not at my odd, misshapen corporeal presence. There is no other me."

The slip itself is part of the understanding here, the error that helps us to register the truth more clearly. All our relatives are dead; it's just Alma and me, no uncles, aunts, cousins on either side. No, there are other kinds of relations, and we don't have those. Hitchcock liked to say that he was celibate, that he was chaste, that he had had sex only once, on the occasion of begetting Pat. Was it true? Almost certainly not, mathematically. But as a matter of general fact over time? Yes, probably. But then the repeated confession is not only a way of saying, "I am my films, my films are me." It also says, "I don't like to talk seriously about this kind of thing, so let's get it out of the way." And more elaborately, by implication, "My knowledge of sexual activity is almost entirely theoretical, a richly protected mental deposit, and in my life and in my films I reap the benefits not of repression but of untouched, unpracticed desire. Why do you think I am so fond of scabrous jokes?"

But then what about Alma? How did she regard all this abstinence? McGilligan suggests she may have felt something stronger than affection for the writer Whitfield Cook, who worked with Hitchcock on *Stage Fright* and *Strangers on a Train,* but he treads very carefully. They spent a lot of time together, and "it appears," McGilligan says, "that they began making love" one evening, but the event was "complicated by an overseas call." The last phrase comes from Cook's diary, and we are left in the dark about the precise stage at which the complication occurred. The couple continued to meet for quite some time after this, but the fling, if that is what it was, was over. The incident suggests a moment of unusual need on Alma's part and reinforces our sense of her discretion and self-discipline at other times. The larger pattern of her life indicates that she had long known just what she was (not) going to get from her marriage, and that whatever Hitchcock's sexual powers were or weren't, his dependence on her ran to extraordinary affective and emotional lengths.

Meanwhile Alma and Alfred Hitchcock had become American citizens (in 1951 and 1955, respectively), and Hitchcock had become an American director. What does this mean? He hadn't lost his English manners or styles of dress. His daughter, Pat, says he lost his accent, as Alma had not, but then as far as I can tell he retrieved it every time he appeared in public. But an important part of a successful immigration is adding a nationality, not giving one up. When Vladimir Nabokov's character Pnin says he too will be an American soon, the context suggests a rather plaintive joke: How could he be anything other than the comic, displaced Russian we know? The subtler point is that he could be American and remain just that person: This is part of what "America" means. Hitchcock was an American director not only because he took America as his subject so often, but because he explored American preoccupations, made them his own — or more precisely, devoted his time and imagination to them while retaining, in several corners of his mind, a fidelity to quite different, more settled un-American versions of reality. He wasn't new to being slightly outside the world he lived in; that was how he lived in England.

To think of the Paramount films is to think of a brilliant VistaVision effect that at first sight seems to be at odds with Hitchcock's dark world; a high color mood, we might say, that went beyond the simple shift from black and white that Hitchcock had already made several times. This impression is particularly true of *To Catch a Thief,* one of the most lighthearted of Hitchcock's films, but we also get it from *Rear Window* and the second *Man Who Knew Too Much* — even, although strangely tinted, from *Vertigo.* It's not that color in itself lightens a mood, although adepts of film noir might try to persuade us that it does. In Hitchcock's case it gives a sense of luxury to the show, of expense not spared, and when terrible things happen in this rich and ample world they happen as if they themselves were luxuries, the best of their kind. So that if "Hitchcock" meant the shadows and angles and expressionist lighting of *The Lodger, Shadow of a Doubt,* and *Notorious,* it now also came to mean glittering costumes, sunshine, glamour — and suspicion, mistaken identity, obsession, danger, and death, as the other films had. Hitchcock had not abandoned his old preoccupations, but he had found a new playground for them, and this elaborate playground is the scene of perhaps his greatest movies. When he moved from Paramount to MGM for *North by Northwest,* he took his ideas of color with him, or rather he took everything we suppose the color of the films of this period may represent. In this context the Hitchcock films with a documentary look, especially *I Confess* and *The Wrong Man,* seem to be striking achievements belonging to another man with the same name — a third man, so to speak, neither the old expressionist nor the new color artist. They are good, modest movies, but their more vivid companions make them look like brief trips down a road not otherwise taken. This would be a way of saying that a certain extravagance, an interest in baroque possibilities rather than sturdy probabilities, had become part of Hitchcock's signature: not what he had to go for or all he had to go for, but what he went for better than anyone else.

6

High Anxieties

Portrait of an Obsession

ERTIGO WAS NOT a hit when it appeared in 1958.
Most critics and viewers found it slow and far-fetched.
And then it vanished from view for a while, since it was
one of the five films Hitchcock personally owned (the others
were *Rear Window, The Trouble with Harry, Rope,* and the second version of *The Man Who Knew Too Much*), and he chose to
take them all out of circulation. Until 1983, your only chance of
a sight of them was a pirated copy, a visit to the Cinémathèque
Française in Paris, a stint on the Steenbeck editing machine
at the Library of Congress in Washington, DC, or a similar
adventure.

On *Vertigo*'s reappearance the consensus was quite different.
By this time Hitchcock had entered the pantheon of great directors, but also something in the film now spoke to the times,
something that had either not been perceptible in 1958 or didn't
quite belong there. Very soon the film was seen as not just good
but great, and in 2012 it displaced *Citizen Kane* at the top of the
British film magazine *Sight and Sound*'s chart of the best films
of all time. *Kane* slipped to second place after fifty years at number one.

One reason why the portrait of an obsession might in time
overtake the portrait of an ambition — to say nothing of the
other ingredients of these two remarkable movies — is that obsessions are both unfathomable and unbreakable, and we have

become devoted to representations of what we can't change and can't understand, as we were certainly not in the 1950s. But a narrower and more manageable question might be why the very good novel by the French thriller writers Pierre Boileau and Thomas Narcejac on which the film is based, although stylish and intelligent and inventive, would never be taken for a great work of fiction, though *Vertigo* is thought to be a great movie. Part of the answer would have to do with the medium: You can infect a movie audience with an obsession, but a reader of a novel is more likely just to track it as you describe it and illustrate it. But of course there could be lousy films and great novels about obsessions, so the fuller answer must involve both the medium and what Hitchcock does with it.

The novel in this case expertly does the job it sets out to do; it entertains and mystifies in just the right proportions. The film redefines the very idea of the job it might do. It doesn't get lost, but it mimes the lostness of characters caught between conspiracy and desire, between sobriety and fascination, and leaves us wondering why we care so much about these wavering people. This development is all the more striking because Hitchcock took so much care to get close to the novel and its world before departing from it. He screened Henri-Georges Clouzot's *Les diaboliques,* also based on a Boileau and Narcejac novel, several times for his writers and members of his crew. The twist here was that Clouzot had self-consciously been making a "Hitchcock" film; Hitchcock liked the homage and the result, but was also determined to show that he was someone else — not Clouzot and not even his own old self.

The casting is unusually important here. It matters that James Stewart plays the key male role, and that Hitchcock was not tempted to gloat over Kim Novak as he did over Grace Kelly or Tippi Hedren — he was too annoyed with her. Here as in other films, of course, Stewart brought himself to the picture, lent Hitchcock the imaginary history he had created in other works. But Hitchcock, already in *Rope,* had found in Stewart a darkness that was not supposed to be there, as if his patient, thoughtful manner were not a comfort to him but a quiet mode of torment. The effect fades a little in the second *Man Who Knew Too Much* and in *Rear Window,* where Stewart's calm too easily overcomes his supposed anxiety.

For the first hour or so of *Vertigo,* the film's curious authority, its extraordinary hold on us, arises from a mixture of the implausible and the irresistible. After that, everything changes and all kinds of new questions appear and fail to go away. What's implausible, of course, is the murder plot in which James Stewart as Scottie Ferguson becomes involved. Gavin Elster, Scottie's college friend, has returned to San Francisco from Europe and wants to get rid of his rich wife. And does. No one suspects him, and he returns to Europe an entirely (maritally and legally) free man. So far, so simple. He had an accomplice, but he paid her off and she's not going to make any trouble.

Elster's plot itself, however, is so elaborate and beautifully crafted that it makes the goings-on in Hitchcock's other films look like Naturalism 101. Elster's assistant pretends to be his wife, who conveniently almost never comes into town from their country place. The assistant also pretends to be prey to fugue states in which she is possessed by an ancestress, Carlotta Valdes, who committed suicide in 1857. She visits the unfortunate woman's grave, stares at a portrait of her in the Legion of Honor museum, and finally — notionally age twenty-six, as Carlotta was when she died — flings herself into the bay under the Golden Gate Bridge. Elster has contracted Scottie, a retired police detective, to keep an eye on his wife and preserve her from any harm that may come to her in her possessed state. Scottie dutifully trails her on her visits and her desultory drives around town, and is luckily on hand when she jumps into the bay. Perhaps Elster was counting on Scottie's falling in love with the woman — as his wife she is called Madeleine, later she is called Judy — but he certainly meant him to be fascinated. If he was fascinated he wouldn't have to believe in the possession story, only to believe that she believed in it, and care about it because she did.

Scottie retired from the police force because he was suffering from acute acrophobia brought on by the climax of a chase across the rooftops we saw in the film's opening sequence. The crook gets away, Scottie dangles from a gutter, and the policeman who tries to help him falls to his death. We don't even see how Scottie gets down from his perilous position. In the next shot he is well into his physical recovery. We don't know whether Elster devised his murder plan when he read about Scottie or whether he had the plan and was waiting for a suitable acrophobic stooge — happily, neither possibility approaches plausibility.

Here's the plan: Elster will take his wife to the top of the bell tower of an old mission some way south of San Francisco, kill her, and wait. The false Madeleine will lead Scottie there, run up the stairs — his condition will mean he can't make it all the way to the top — and he will see his Madeleine, or at least an identically dressed woman, fall past a window opening to her death. Some time later, Elster and the false Madeleine will make their escape, leaving the dead wife to the inquest and the afterlife she is not going to have.

All we see though — all we have seen so far — is just what Scottie sees: the apparently possessed wandering woman, the would-be suicide with whom he has of course fallen in love, and the tumbling body. We have been Elster's dupes as much as Scottie is, having, according to Hitchcock, "no idea at all that this is a murder story." And we attend the excruciating inquest with Scottie, where the judge, outside of all probability but in tune with the charged and persecutory landscape of this film, spends all his inquiry not on the woman's death, but on Scottie's weakness and his bad habit of letting people die by dropping from high places.

In its first hour the film co-opts our eyes and ears for Scottie's sense of the world. We don't exactly see what he sees. We see what he would see if he had different eyes (if his eyes were a camera with a zoom lens). We also hear Bernard Herrmann's magnificent score, which Scottie doesn't; although *when* we hear it is even more important than what we hear.

One simple instance and then a more complicated one. Scottie is parked outside of Madeleine's building, looking at her car. We see him looking, and then we get a view from his angle and distance. There seems to be a bouquet on the dashboard, but we are not near enough to be sure. (Nor is Scottie.) Now there is a shot of him peering at the car, shading his eyes, as if he could get closer just by wanting to see. The camera obliges, takes us halfway across the courtyard that separates Scottie from Madeleine's car. Yes, it is a bouquet, the one Madeleine had made up in town as a copy of the one in the painting of Carlotta. Scottie hasn't seen it any better than he did at first, but we have, and we lend our vision to him.

In the other instance Scottie trails Madeleine to the art gallery and watches her looking at the painting of Carlotta. A whole large room separates him from the painting and Madeleine seated in front of it. As he looks the camera zooms in on the bouquet she has beside her on the seat, then continues to the painting, ending on a close-up of a similar bouquet there. We see Scottie again, standing at the same distance, and we cut to a swirl in Madeleine's hairdo, zooming in and then moving on to the same swirl in Carlotta's hair, this time in a close-up that almost puts us into the painting, a visual proximity that Scottie could have achieved only by climbing over Madeleine and using a small ladder. Some version of this effect happens in movies all the time — how often is our vision simply aligned with that of a character? — but here it is truly extravagant. It's not that Scottie can't see what he sees and make his deductions. It's that he can't see it in this way, and our literal viewing becomes a metaphor for what he thinks. He may now believe that Elster's whole story of possession is right, or that Madeleine thinks she is possessed. At least he has to make something of the definitive connection between Madeleine and Carlotta: "Definitive" is what those zooms say. The beauty of this effect, of course, once we know the full story, is that this irrefutable proposition is simply untrue; the proof itself was part of the intricate ensnaring plan. Something is going on here that makes us think about Hitchcock and his camera rather than about Elster's calculations.

There is a sense in which *Vertigo* is so purely a movie — so purely involved in what movies do — that we can almost let the plot go. I don't mean its subject is the movies or moviemaking. I mean it beautifully and scarily exploits the possibilities of the medium, makes our dependence on them something like an addiction. Scottie's plight becomes a kind of conduit for our own absorption. What might have been — and still is, in a certain dimension — our sympathy for him (and anger at him) turns into a troubling complicity with everything that has happened to him.

There is no better example of the creation of this effect than the moment when Scottie first sees Madeleine. He is about to turn down the job of spying on Elster's wife for her own good — not his line at all — when Elster says he should see her before he says no. The couple is having dinner at Ernie's restaurant that evening; Scottie could catch a glimpse of her there. Scottie murmurs the name of the restaurant, and as Professor Charles Barr notes in his BFI Film Classics book on *Vertigo,* "We will not hear another word spoken for more than ten minutes." There is a dissolve from Elster's office to the entrance of Ernie's, and the next shot shows Scottie sitting at the bar. The camera moves along the bar to the left, not following Scottie's line of vision but the shape of the room. There are lots of diners. The dark red wallpaper is very striking, and there's a sense of being inside a magic box. Finally the camera finds Elster sitting at the far side of the restaurant, facing us. His dinner partner is a blonde, but all we see of her apart from her hair is a lavish dark-green-and-black stole that hangs behind her and reaches to the floor. At this point Herrmann's music starts — a full orchestra playing the great swooning *Vertigo* theme, the tune that bespeaks romantic madness, the falling motion you can't wait to make — and the camera moves in slowly toward them. There is a cut to Scottie at the bar looking at them from across the room. Then Elster and his partner get up and walk toward us. Now we see her face. It is Kim Novak as Madeleine, looking slightly unearthly as befits the role Elster wants her to play. She passes Scottie at the bar; he glances at her uncomfortably, turns his head away. As he does this she stands there for a long moment, posing in profile: sheer mystery, but surely too serene to be crazy — an effect Novak gets as perhaps no one else could. Of course, here again, we are seeing what Scottie doesn't see so steadily. Elster and the false Madeleine leave. Scottie sits at the bar for a little while, and in the next scene he has started his surveillance job; he is waiting outside her building. Scottie will follow this woman around for any reason, for no reason, since he is the victim, as we are, of costume, decor, music, physical beauty, lighting, camera movements, and, of course, impeccable timing.

This mood reaches its climax in a series of shots often used in advertisements for the film. Scottie and Madeleine are in love with each other now, and he's not thinking about the job he is doing for Elster beyond wanting to save her from her madness; she is not thinking of anything except the horrible plot she has to carry through to the end. They stand in front of a rather cheaply back-projected ocean, which somehow makes the scene more convincing rather than less — their romance, as the lyricist Lorenz Hart might say, doesn't need a blue lagoon standing by, or a sea that looks less movie-made. They embrace as if there were no one else in the world, no story in the world, nowhere to go, nowhere to have been. The music is important, since it repeats the theme that runs throughout the film. It keeps time but doesn't recognize time; it will always come back as long as there are people ready to forget everything except each other and their emotions. The cadences from Wagner don't do any harm here. And the madness will include us, since we are the ones listening to the music.

But soon Scottie and Madeleine find their way to the mission, and Elster's plot plays out just as it should. As far as Scottie is concerned, Madeleine is dead. He is desolate, hospitalized, and another spectacular moment occurs, this time involving his friend Midge (Barbara Bel Geddes). She has been visiting him in his room, playing Mozart to him on the record player — the perfect therapy music, she has been told. He pays no attention to it, or to her and her brave, kindly jokes. She goes to see his doctor. On the way there she walks briskly down the corridor, straight down the middle. When she leaves the doctor's room, defeated by his idiotic analysis of Scottie's condition, and by her own realization of how far he is from anything resembling psychic health, she stays very close to the right-hand wall, almost leaning on it, walking very slowly. Cellos accompany her down the corridor, as if they were the voice of mourning and departure. When she gets to the end of the corridor she pauses, a figure made tiny by distance. She doesn't leave; we abandon her in a slow fade to black. We never see her again, and we realize that this is one of Hitchcock's good-byes: He never lets a character he cares about make a final exit without a visual farewell. This scene is in some ways a counterpart to the one in which Scottie first sees Madeleine. Midge has understood that Scottie's infatu-

ation is irredeemable, that Madeleine's death can only eternal-
ize it. Her shaky departure leaves us to live with the condition
we helped him to create. It's like saying good-bye to sanity, and
when Scottie leaves the hospital he is twice shown on a street
next to a sign that says "One Way."

And then things change — Charles Barr writes of "the her-
metic intensity of the final 40 minutes." Scottie is now really
possessed by a dead woman in the way that the woman he knew
as Madeleine was only pretending to be. Even when he's out of
the hospital and looking reasonably recovered, if distinctly glum,
he sees her everywhere: in a woman in a gray suit, a woman in a
white coat. As they get closer he realizes they look nothing like
Madeleine. Here as earlier Hitchcock creates a delicate divorce
between the story we almost unconsciously construct and what
we actually see. On one of the occasions of Scottie's eager error,
the person who looks like Madeleine *is* Kim Novak, replaced by
another actress in the later, nearer shot. We correct the picture
and attribute the misidentification to Scottie's delusion. But we
were not actually deluded — we just happened to be following
the delusion's line of vision.

So the fantastic fiction becomes the psychological truth;
possession is possible. But Elster's fiction, in spite or because
of its dazzling complication, always had unruly edges, and the
false Madeleine has not left town, as any smart accomplice to
a murder would have done. She is now living in a hotel under
her own name, Judy Barton, and Scottie catches sight of her
one day on the street. Does he recognize her? No, but he sees
something. Our own dizziness here, or mine at least, is more or
less out of control. I know this is Kim Novak, and not just because I've seen the film before. I've seen her in other films and
other costumes; this is Kim Novak. At the same time and on
a quite different imaginative wavelength, I think this person is
not Madeleine, doesn't look at all like Madeleine, and Scottie
is crazy to think he sees a resemblance. As Tania Modleski says,

"she looks 'wrong,' a disappointing counterfeit of the beautiful Madeleine." But then why am I so sure it's the same actress if I'm also sure he's got the wrong woman?

I don't know the answer to this question, and of course it becomes moot as soon as Scottie and Judy start talking. This is where Hitchcock chooses to let us in on the plot, the murder story. Alone after a first conversation with Scottie (first as far as he is concerned), Judy decides to leave town and then decides to stay. Hitchcock treats us to a flashback of the end of the scene at the mission: Elster's wife flung off the tower; Madeleine's scream, which is her one act of noncomplicity; their escape. The novel keeps this revelation until the end, and Hitchcock's alteration has been much discussed. "Everyone around me was against this change," Hitchcock said. It makes for a clumsy interruption of narrative and sudden inconsistency of point of view, but it achieves in the strongest terms an effect Hitchcock never stopped seeking: the destruction of mystery and the creation of suspense, which is always a matter of knowing what happens but not what the consequences will be.

Scottie wants to improve on what he takes to be Judy's resemblance to Madeleine, and the process ends in what the director Chris Marker describes as "the most magical camera movement that remains the most magical in the whole history of cinema." She accepts the makeover and we see her in a misty green light — the effect of the neon sign outside the window of her hotel room. The message is clear: She has turned into a ghost; Scottie has turned her into a ghost. Then she steps forward into a brighter, whiter light. No, not a ghost, and not even Judy transformed: just Madeleine, resurrection and nothing else, even if we remember that this miracle is for her merely the adoption of an earlier costume and hairdo. In fact, this banality, the distance from means to end, may enhance the huge effect. The long, rapturous embrace that follows, with the room seeming to circle around the two lovers, is a great movie clincher, and has provoked critics to think of the story of Tristan and Isolde. Here, however, love is not death but the cancellation of death, and the identity of the lovers, along with their whole story, almost disappears into this apotheosis.

Not for long, though, because the film, as if apologizing for its flight into metaphysics, quickly returns to its plot and the exposure of deceit. Judy foolishly (or boldly, looking for a showdown) puts on the necklace she wore as Madeleine. Scottie spots it, grasps at once the accomplished fancy plan, and drags her off to the mission. He hauls her up the stairs of the bell tower, hoping to throw off his acrophobia through his anger and other emotions, and of course to torture her as much as possible. It's worth noting that in these scenes Hitchcock manages to turn James Stewart into a real, grimacing villain, something I would not have believed possible if I had not seen him do it in *The Man Who Knew Too Much,* in which Stewart, as a doctor, brutally administers a drug to his wife rather than tell her the bad news he has learned. These scenes are not pleasant, but they are an achievement, both for the actor and the director.

The end of *Vertigo* is so incidental and contrived it can only come from some impulse behind the story rather than anything in its logic. A nun appears in the bell tower, presumably wondering who these people are, and Judy, startled, steps back and falls to her death. Scottie can't have wanted her dead; he was just indulging in his outrage, avenging his degraded love. We can't know what else he wanted because Judy's death scoops him back into the pattern that has been established since the beginning of the film and that has nothing to do with human motives or wishes. The recurring situations in the film begin to look as if they compose an obscure fable about fatal falls from high places, and the person who is left helplessly watching each time they happen. In the novel there is talk of allowing someone to die in our place, as if anyone who has died *near* us has died *for* us. This isn't quite the feeling of the movie. In *Vertigo* it's as if just having people die near you, especially if it happens three times, is itself a form of fate, a definition of who you are.

Speculations

Men and women die in proximity to Scottie, but the death or danger of a woman is a dominant feature in almost all of Hitchcock's films. Women are threatened in every killer film he made and actually murdered in several. Ingrid Bergman is poisoned in *Notorious,* young Charlie has no real idea of what she is getting into in *Shadow of a Doubt,* and the heroine of *North by Northwest* is a double agent who has been uncloaked by the enemy. The heroines of *Blackmail* and *Sabotage* narrowly escape the clutches of the law.

Key moments in these danger stories often have especially brilliant camera effects, and Chabrol and Rohmer say of the shots of Bergman in *Notorious,* when her character has been poisoned, that "the whole screen glitters with the indescribable beauty of which Hitchcock found the secret in [expressionist film director F. W.] Murnau." This is a little rhapsodic but picks up on something that takes us beyond the individual movies. That something is surely autobiographical in some way.

Is it sadism, as the dark view of Hitchcock proclaims, a pleasure in seeing beautiful women in harm's way? The solitary joy of the otherwise uxorious director? A revenge on the mother the child thought might leave him forever? There may be a piece of the truth here as far as the late films and Hitchcock's relation with Tippi Hedren are concerned. He himself made jokes about his supposed sadism, but that practice can play either way: as an effective lighthearted denial or an unmistakable indirect confession. Still, the thought doesn't take us very far into the films or Hitchcock's affective life, and John Russell Taylor's theory is more persuasive.

His suggestion is that far from enjoying the torments of these women at risk, Hitchcock identified with them. He *was* these women on some wavelength of the morbid or flustered imagination. Ingrid Bergman, *c'est moi*. Taylor goes a little far in his refusal of the idea of sadism — all the way to its opposite or complement. Hitchcock was "entirely at home, and I think happiest, in the company of women," he writes, and "his role in the films was masochistic rather than, as so frequently claimed, sadistic." I'm not sure how we get from home and company to masochism — it depends on our tastes, I guess — but a slightly more oblique version of this thought makes good sense to me.

Hitchcock was a frightened man who got his fears to work for him on film. Those fears, in reality and on film, took many forms, but dramatically and emotionally they needed a carrier, a representative, and that representative was by preference a woman in danger. The women in the movies, we might say — this is a little hard on real women and real actresses who have non-symbolic lives of their own to live — are whatever we most fear to lose, the persons whose imaginary death would cost us most. Isn't it masochism to linger over them? It could be. But it could also just be an act of thinking the worst ("one has to consider all possibilities"), an act of propitiation to the gods who take these treasures away.

The intimate sense of Hitchcock himself lurking in *Vertigo* arises, I suggest, from a different source: from the fact that he is both Elster and Scottie, both the smooth, fantastic plotter and the hallucinating accomplice and victim. Because, of course, Hitchcock had other fears apart from those of losing what he most cared about. He was afraid of being wrong, being tricked, of trusting in reason, of being too clever, of not being clever enough, and above all of having made a mistake in devoting his life to the technological reproduction of dreams. Every new film was an attempt to dispel the idea of this mistake. When he joked about the relationship between his own job and his father's, he wasn't entirely joking. "Though I am in no way a gambler by nature," he said, "the endeavor I have chosen as my life's work has put me in a position not so different from that of my father — a speculator in perishables." Of course he was also happy making films. He loved many of his inventions and he knew how good he was. He knew there was no long-term mistake. But that is the Hitchcock who created *Vertigo,* not the speculator who hides among its perishable frames.

Can't Say It Is

Hitchcock had an idea while he was making *North by Northwest.* "Have you ever seen an assembly line?" he asked Truffaut, who replied that he hadn't. Hitchcock continued:

> They're absolutely fantastic. Anyway, I wanted to have a long dialogue scene between Cary Grant and one of the factory workers as they walk along the assembly line. They might, for instance, be talking about one of the foremen. Behind them a car is being assembled, piece by piece. Finally, the car they've seen being put together from a simple nut and bolt is complete, with gas and oil, and all ready to drive off the line. The two men look at it and say, "Isn't it wonderful!" Then they open the door of the car and out drops a corpse! ... Where has the body come from? Not from the car, obviously, since they've seen it start at zero! The corpse falls out of nowhere, you see!

The corpse falls out of nowhere. This might be a kind of motto. Things keep happening in Hitchcock films that are wildly improbable if not downright impossible, but also, mysteriously, just what we expected. This double effect is very powerful because it is so remote from our lives and so close to our nerves. The story lines in Hitchcock, the assembly lines so to speak, all his concessions to plot and probability, seem to be there to give us a faint feel of movie rationality, a hint of the rug before he pulls it away.

But our response suggests almost exactly the reverse. We are delighted to give rationality and realism a break — that's what we came to the movies for. The question is how the impossible can feel so normal, and does this happen only in Hitchcock films? No, it happens every day, but not in our sensible renderings of what the everyday is supposed to look like. The ordinary is not the opposite of the extraordinary; it is where the extraordinary hides, with our timid complicity. And vice versa. "If the story had involved vultures, or birds of prey," Hitchcock said of Daphne du Maurier's "The Birds" — the short story on which the film is based — "I might not have wanted it. The basic appeal to me is that it had to do with ordinary, everyday birds. Do you see what I mean?" We do, we do. As long as the ordinary birds do extraordinary things. Otherwise we'll settle for vultures behaving like sparrows.

The corpse from nowhere also tells us something about the MacGuffin, a device that Hitchcock frequently used and loved to talk about. When I was a child, the local Midland form of the MacGuffin story went like this: Two men are sitting on a railway train passing through England (or sometimes Scotland or Wales). One of them is crumpling up pages of newspaper and throwing them out the window. The other man finally cannot contain his curiosity and asks the first man what he is doing. He says, "Oh, this keeps the elephants away." The second man says, "But there are no elephants in England (or Scotland or Wales)." The first man says, "See." Hitchcock tells Truffaut an almost identical version of the story: Some childhoods are full of bad jokes.

Dictionary definitions note the gimmicky narrative function of the MacGuffin and Hitchcock sometimes spoke of the device in this way ("the mechanical element that usually crops up in any story"). More often he went for its subversive hint of rational nonsense or plausible unreason, the impersonation of self-evident truth. See? The corpse can't have come from nowhere, and there aren't any elephants. What more do we want?

In 1956 Hitchcock had signed up for a project with MGM, a film based on Hammond Innes's *The Wreck of the* Mary Deare, and began work on a treatment with Ernest Lehman, perhaps the subtlest and certainly the funniest of the writers Hitchcock collaborated with. There were many distractions. Lehman, who had written *Sabrina* for Billy Wilder and just finished an adaptation of his own book, *Sweet Smell of Success,* had other jobs to do. Hitchcock had problems to iron out with the shooting of *Vertigo* and a hernia operation to get over too. Somewhere amid these delays Hitchcock returned to an old movie idea he thought of as "The Man in Lincoln's Nose." Lehman was delighted. Did the studio executives oppose the switch? They didn't care; they had Hitchcock, and they liked the look of the two-page outline called "In a Northwesterly Direction." Hitchcock formally began work on the film, still tagged with this title, in June 1958.

"Here, you see," Hitchcock said to Truffaut, "the MacGuffin has been boiled down to its purest expression: nothing at all!" We note the O in the name of Roger O. Thornhill, the bewildered, stylish character played by Cary Grant, and it's clear that the whole plot revolves around confusion between this zero of a man and someone who doesn't exist. Mistaken identity times two: Thornhill isn't this person, and this person isn't anyone. We can tell Hitchcock and Lehman are having a good time, even if we are still trying to work out what to do with the apparent near resurrection of David O. Selznick in the character's name. Or indeed the word "rot" that our man's initials spell out. In any event, it's clear that this zero represents a curious and extreme reiteration of Hitchcock's plea for the individual life. Even a nobody, it turns out, has rights and runs risks. Even in a film about nothing.

North by Northwest starts in a way that defines its terms with extraordinary elegance, asking us to think about design and daily reality together, as if it's easy to fade from one to the other and back. Saul Bass's abstract credit sequence — green screen, credits running across multiple diagonal lines — dissolves into Hitchcock's (briefly, at the start) realistic movie as the lines become the floors of a glass skyscraper full of reflections of cars on a New York City street: Madison Avenue, as it happens, crowded with people, including Hitchcock himself narrowly missing a bus. Thornhill appears, dictating notes to his secretary. They start to walk uptown, then take a taxi. He gets out at the Plaza, meets some business associates in the Oak Room.

Then everything shifts into an entirely different register, apparently for plot reasons, but really because we are beginning to leave all ordinary ideas of plot behind and the pure MacGuffin kicks in. It's instructive that Hitchcock, according to Lehman, talked a lot about the logic of the plot of this movie — in part presumably because of his repeated and gleeful offenses against the very notion of logic.

Getting up to send a telegram, Thornhill is mistaken for a man who is being paged, one George Kaplan. Thornhill is promptly kidnapped and taken off to a palatial pad on Long Island, where after failing to reveal to his interrogators what he is supposed to know about certain operations of the FBI, he is filled with bourbon and dumped in a car rolling downhill. Half asleep and fully drunk, he nearly drives the car off a cliff but recovers, narrowly misses hitting several cars, has a bad fit of double vision, and finally brakes hard in order to avoid an elderly cyclist. The police car that has been following him for a while crashes into him, and another vehicle crashes into the police car. Thornhill is taken off to the police station, miraculously unharmed but still very drunk. When he tells the story of his kid-napping, no one believes him. This is the kind of movie where an arrested man makes his one phone call not to his lawyer but to his mother. He tells her to bring his lawyer.

So far so random. Hitchcock said that at this point in the shooting of the film even Grant didn't know what was going on. Of course various snippy questions may have started to tip-toe across our minds. If we wanted to question a man we had picked up in Manhattan, why would we take him out to Long Island? Is turning a man into a drunken driver the best way of killing him? Does no one care about how terrible the back pro-jection is — couldn't Hitchcock have done better than the mani-fest movie of a road scrolling behind Grant's studio-based head?

In fact, once you have begun to glimpse what Hitchcock is up to, even the mundane suspicions represented by these questions begin to work for him. Hitchcock has no interest in New York geography or practical murder or plausible criminal thinking or perfected screen illusion. It's not that he doesn't care about reality, just that the reality he cares about is in the haunted mind and not in the imitable world. When we look again at the drunk-driving scene, we see not a ham-fisted drama of suspense — will Thornhill get out of this alive? — but a to-tally persuasive picture of a man in the grip of a nightmare, our nightmare, the car and the life terminally out of control. All we see really is Thornhill's face, and it's all we need to see. He blinks, stares, frowns, squints, leans forward, leans back, almost falls asleep. He is driving and not driving. He doesn't know what he's doing but he's doing what he can.

This effect, and this narrative logic, is even clearer in the movie's most famous scene, although the nightmare is differ-ent. Thornhill takes a bus out of Chicago to a place on a lonely, dusty road where he is supposed to meet the man he is supposed to be. The audience knows, although he doesn't, that Kaplan doesn't exist, that he is a phantom agent constructed by the

CIA to throw the bad guys off the scent of the real agent. The bad guys, however, still think Thornhill is Kaplan and are determined to kill him. And here again our dim, obvious questions get us further into Hitchcock's world than they seem to have any promise of doing. Is this any way to get rid of a troublesome opponent? Send him on an hour-and-a-half bus journey and attack him from a crop-dusting plane? Why isn't he in Chicago? There is a whole history of more efficient disposals there.

The scene on the road is magnificent, worth seeing again and again. Thornhill gets off the bus and waits. This is not just the middle of nowhere; it is the Platonic idea of such a place. A couple of cars pass, a truck. Then an old car trundles out of a field and deposits a man in a suit. The car turns around and vanishes. Is this Kaplan? Thornhill walks uncertainly across the road and asks him if Kaplan is his name. Succinctly combining truth and reason, the man replies, "Can't say it is, 'cause it ain't." Then just before the bus he's been waiting for arrives he remarks, "That's funny." Thornhill says, "What?" The man says, "That plane's dustin' crops where there ain't no crops." He leaves on the bus. The plane zooms in to attack Thornhill and the rest is movie history, part of the iconography of loneliness and the risk of death in America. As the philosopher Stanley Cavell notes in his book *The World Viewed: Reflections on the Ontology of Film,* "*Of course* the Great Plains is a region in which men are unprotected from the sky." It's not just the sky, though, it's also the empty earth. Cavell speaks of the uncanny in relation to this scene, which points us exactly where we need to go — or where Hitchcock is going. The uncanny is the reappearance of the familiar in the shape of the alien: That's why most of the time we fail to be sufficiently surprised by it, as suggested by Cavell's "of course." But we are surprised, even if insufficiently, and the "of course" comes late. The whole point of repression is that it works and doesn't work. The attacking plane is not an arbitrary bit of movie action, or rather that's just what it is and why the scene sticks in the mind. As arbitrary action, it represents what has to happen in the world of our fears.

There is a remarkable scene in the film in which the characters and the script actually confess their interest in these displays — their own commitment, so to speak, to Hitchcock's movie and to everyone's nightmares. The villain, Phillip Vandamm (James Mason), reproaches Thornhill: "Has anyone ever told you that you overplay your various roles rather severely, Mr. Kaplan?" Vandamm lists the roles and concludes: "It seems to me you fellows could stand a little less training from the FBI and a little more from the Actors Studio." Thornhill, not to be left out of the metaphor or the irony, says, "Apparently the only performance that will satisfy you is when I play dead." Vandamm replies without the least emphasis, "Your very next role." Thornhill, undaunted, says, "I wonder what subtle form of manslaughter is next on the program." These elaborate designs and the reference to them may seem gratuitous, but of course that is precisely the point. As Hitchcock told Truffaut, "Even a gratuitous scene must have some justification for being there, you know."

Out of Luck

A Little Mad

WHEN HITCHCOCK TOLD Charlotte Chandler that to interview him she would have to interview his films, he was mainly joking. She was certainly not rising to the challenge and said she had already done that but they wouldn't tell her their secrets. They didn't tell me either, but I find them full of takes on the world, full of radical, provocative thoughts about how to live in it and interpret it, about what to be afraid of and where we might place our trust, if such a thing was possible. They portray societies that don't know themselves, that don't know enough about knowledge; and they shift, with Hitchcock's move to America, from pictures of a beleaguered, blinkered, dangerous world to pictures of a confident, experimental, yet still dangerous one.

In Ben Macintyre's biography of the notorious spy Kim Philby, *A Spy Among Friends,* we learn that a friend bought Philby's wife a ticket for a London showing of *The Birds*. This was perhaps, the writer speculates, the friend's "way of warning" her that "a life that seems calm and secure can swiftly turn to nightmare." A rather oblique warning, and there are conclusions one could draw from that film that have a closer relation to the world of espionage, or at least the state of siege represented by the Cold War. But it is true that Hitchcock's late films, from *Psycho* onward, are all about the turn to nightmare in a way that his earlier films were not. Or perhaps we should say that nightmare flickers frequently in the earlier work, while in the later movies it comes to stay, takes over the world.

The change almost certainly has to do with Hitchcock's television work and self-presentation in that medium, and his changing sense of audience. The television audience feels closer in many ways; Hitchcock talks directly to it, plays games with it, and he clearly feels the need to manipulate its reactions more thoroughly than he could those of a cinema audience — or indeed perhaps could want to. For these and other reasons *Psycho* looks, in the best sense, like a long television show made for a movie audience, and part of its shock lies in the sheer domesticity of what it shows: not just the famous shower but the toilet in the same bathroom, apparently the first toilet ever seen in a Hollywood film. And the whole first section of the movie in which Marion Crane (Janet Leigh) tries to break free from her unhappy life by stealing some money and joining her lover has a weird humdrum banality about it that is unusual for a genre movie. It's as if *Frankenstein,* or better still *Young Frankenstein,* had been shot as if it were a television documentary.

Of course all this is the setup for the horrors of the shower scene, where Norman Bates (Anthony Perkins), impersonating his mother, brutally stabs Marion, and part of the lurid urgency of this scene rests on the ordinariness of what goes before it. But the ordinariness has its own continuing authority. Much of this effect comes from the strange insistence, in the first part of the film, on the camera's possibilities as an agent of invasion. It creeps up to a window that is open a little at the bottom, pauses, and then slips through the opening to spy on Marion and her lover. It looks around Marion's room at the motel, checking out all the furniture, focusing on the newspaper in which she has hidden the stolen money. It does the same when Norman is cleaning up the mess he made by the killing. Cameras perform this sort of role in movies all the time, of course; but they don't always make us feel like spies, and they don't always have such fussy patience with the mundane. That last spot of blood on the side of the bathtub ... is Norman going to catch it and wipe it away? Of course he is. We do have a little technical background here too. Stephen Rebello, the author of *Alfred Hitchcock and the Making of* Psycho, tells us: "The director insisted on cameraman John Russell's shooting virtually the entire movie with 50-millimeter lenses. On the 35-millimeter cameras of the day, such lenses gave the closest approximation to human vision technically possible."

But of course Hitchcock could have felt the world actually was turning into a nightmare, and if so the effect of *Psycho* would have nothing to do with a different use of the medium. David Thomson has another word for what I am calling ordinariness: "nastiness," which he defines as "a noir disillusionment with the dream of happiness" that "was about to overtake not just the American movie but the nation's way of life." He says, "It is remarkable how many glimpses Alfred Hitchcock allows of a grasping, devious, and ordinarily nasty nation ... The central killing grows out of the grim unkindness of the world we have seen ..." Things must be a little more complicated (and less allegorical) than this, but the film does pull off an apparently impossible social and psychological coup. It invites us to be violently surprised by a totally exceptional event, the act that converts the small-time love and crime story into a horror movie, and also to wonder whether this exception not only proves the rule but, in some sort of deviant, figurative way, *is* the rule. This is why the wonderful conversation Marion has with Norman before he kills her is so important. Its amiable low-grade philosophizing has us all nodding our heads in agreement without any idea of what we are agreeing to. "We're all in our private traps," Norman says, and Marion thinks he's right — she's just about to abandon her attempt to get out of her trap. And although his mother is ill, he says, "It's not like she was a maniac, a raving thing. She just goes a little mad sometimes. We all go a little mad sometimes." How true. We all do. And then we disguise ourselves as our mothers and kill someone. Having killed our mother some time ago, of course.

In earlier Hitchcock films this slippage from the ordinary to the terrifying, the turn to nightmare, is always a possibility, but the possibility is the subject: the fear or delusion, the obsession, the possession by the uncanny. Here as in the later movies — *The Birds* and *Marnie* especially — what is possible is what bluntly, violently happens, and Hitchcock, "changed more than he could have guessed," has become a maker of a different kind of movie. In *Psycho,* as in *Strangers on a Train,* everything depends on a chance encounter, except that here the heroine is dead. Hitchcock had a kind of reprieve when he learned that audiences at screenings of *Psycho* were laughing as well as screaming, and from then on he claimed to have had his tongue in his cheek all along. I'm sure that's where his tongue was but his work wasn't now suggesting that effect. Anthony Perkins said he thought that Hitchcock was uncertain about the tone of the film, and that his reaction to the news of laughter in the audience was one of surprise: "He was confused, at first, incredulous second, and despondent third."

Many other factors intervened, of course, apart from the translation of the television experience to film: Hitchcock's health, the end of the studio system, changing tastes, a new generation of actors. And many of us are very fond of certain of Hitchcock's late films. *The Birds* and *Frenzy* have their ardent admirers, and I am about to claim that *Family Plot* is seriously underrated. Everyone who has seen *Frenzy* remembers the slow tracking shot down the stairs and away from an apartment where a woman is going to be killed. It is both an eloquent homage to the woman, whom we shan't see alive again, and who has earned our sympathy by believing, against all the odds, that the innocent man is innocent, and a sinister suggestion of how fine and private murder is, since the camera pulls away down the corridor and into the street, which is so busy and noisy that even the loudest screams for help are not going to be heard. But *Marnie, Topaz,* and *Torn Curtain* look like films made by a Hitchcock clone who wasn't concentrating, and photographs of Hitchcock at this time show him looking tired and sad, his face blotched and anxious, the whole image a long way from the old imitation of portly, unruffled pride. Even *The Birds,* with its genuinely magnificent moments, and its admirable refusal to explain what it is actually about, looks for much of the time like an imitation of one of its 1950s predecessors. The large point, however, has to do with the shift represented by *Psycho,* and the end of the film offers a sort of parable of what is happening in his work.

Norman kills a detective who is looking for Marion and is about to kill Marion's sister — Norman is dressed up as his mother each time — when Marion's lover, who is helping the sister in her search, arrives and disarms him in the nick of time. The next scene is a police station, where the sister and the lover, several policemen, and a few officials are all waiting to hear what the psychiatrist has to say about Norman's condition. Why do they need to hear this, and why do they sit so patiently through the "psychological analysis" he spouts after he's interviewed his patient?

There are various possibilities here. Perhaps Hitchcock was just nervous about the Motion Picture Production Code, as McGilligan suggests. Perhaps he worried about his audience's comprehension of the difficult idea of the split personality and collaborated too eagerly with his writer on the film, Joseph Stefano, in telling us more than we need to know about how Norman believed he was his mother, and the mother part of him was jealous of the other part, and so on. These explanations of Hitchcock's choice are unlikely, because he was an expert at getting around the Production Code, and even if he had lost some of his own old obliquity, he couldn't have lost it all.

What's more, the reasoning doesn't account for the marvelously obnoxious performance by Simon Oakland as the psychiatrist (a year later he was the unpleasant Lieutenant Schrank in *West Side Story*). The scene is a dark joke of some kind, and not unlike many of the jokes Hitchcock made in his television series, parading obvious bits of information as if he didn't know how obvious they were. The joke no doubt misfires, but its point is pretty clear. Hitchcock hasn't lost his old obliquity; he has decided to go for a direct attack on our stupidity. When he was working on *Sabotage,* Hitchcock used to joke with the writer Peter Viertel about his audiences as "the moron masses," but in the film itself the phrase is given to an American admirer of the Nazis. What *Psycho* lacks is this ironic displacement. It is a powerful film and a perfect instance of the later Hitchcock. But for those of us who are devoted to the complexities and secrets of *Vertigo,* the elegance and wit of *North by Northwest,* it can seem very blunt.

Old Tricks

We may wonder whether in his sixties (in life and in his movies) Hitchcock is not replaying, too clumsily now, some of his old well-publicized tricks. As a boy he pinned a firecracker to a schoolmate's pants. As an adult he bet a property man that he wouldn't dare to spend a night alone in the studio, handcuffed to a camera, and offered the fellow a bottle of brandy to see him through. The brandy was spiked with laxative, and the man was found weeping in the morning, his clothes soiled, more exhausted by his humiliation than by his vigil. We have to worry about the person (and the culture) able to find this prank funny — and the fact that the story has become part of the lore of British cinema, cited not only by Hitchcock biographers but also in the memoirs of others, could well be part of our worry.

Alas, even this appalling trick had a strange sequel. A friend tried the brandy-with-laxative trick on Hitchcock himself, offering a bottle as a thank-you gift. There were no visible effects, and Hitchcock did not mention the matter further. Finally, the friend could stand the uncertainty no longer and asked Hitchcock if he had enjoyed the brandy. "Oh, yes," Hitchcock said, "I didn't want to mention it, but my mother is ill, and when the doctor prescribed brandy, we gave her some of yours." The guilt-stricken friend sent flowers and sympathy to Hitchcock's mother, only to discover she was perfectly fit and knew nothing of any brandy.

Practical jokes in bad taste were very common in Hitchcock's England, and it makes sense to see in them, as many people have, a strangled desire to communicate and a wish for mastery in miniature over a world that seems unruly in its ordinary dimensions. But I wonder whether their principal purpose is not more disruptive, a turning of all transactions to mischief and disorder. In England these jokes suggest — or used to suggest — not aggression finding an outlet in humor, but an impulse toward anarchy that civilized people can hardly confess in any other way. And that Hitchcock in particular could scarcely bear to think he had.

But Hitchcock's jokes are not merely an aspect of his Englishness, and they are not a little hobby, as I suppose he thought they were, or a projection of some snarled Dostoyevskian cobweb in his brain, as Donald Spoto implies. They are companion pieces to his films, which also deal in planned, short-term disturbances of the ordinary, disciplined flirtations with the unpredictable. Celebrating his forty-third birthday in Hollywood, Hitchcock stood up after dinner and held a carving knife to his throat, as if to slit it. Then he put the knife away and ordered drinks all around. Spoto finds this an "unusually macabre display," and certainly the gag is in terrible taste. But it is in the same taste as many moments in his movies, and looks like a joke about what a sudden reminder of mortality will do to people, the thought of death as a means of shaking the rituals of our comfort.

But then Hitchcock's treatment of Tippi Hedren during the shooting of *The Birds* was no sort of joke. He confessed to feeling edgy and out of control at this time. He said to Truffaut: "I ran into some emotional problems . . . I was pouring myself into the girl, you know . . . And I got into a state of distress about this." In the final scene of the film the creatures attack the heroine. At first, artificial birds were tried, but they didn't look right, so live birds were attached to Hedren's clothes, and the shooting went on for a week, with the actress and the birds becoming increasingly hysterical. Finally a bird went for Hedren's eyes, and she collapsed. Hitchcock was visibly nervous but insistent. He wanted to shoot this scene, the writer Evan Hunter said, "but something in him didn't want to shoot it." Working with Hedren on his next film, *Marnie*, Hitchcock the timid, according to Spoto, made a sexual proposition to her, accompanied by threats, and was turned down. After that, he wouldn't speak to Hedren or use her name. Taylor says they had an argument about whether she could have a weekend off from the production and reported Hitchcock saying that she had referred, sin of sins, to his weight.

What happened was that Hitchcock fell in love with the star he had created — films and life are unequivocal about what the French critic Bruno Villien calls the Pygmalion gesture, and it is the oldest cliché of Hitchcock criticism, the icy blonde brought to life by love and violence. In Sacha Gervasi's film *Hitchcock* the cliché is crisply rehashed when the characters Vera Miles and Janet Leigh compare directors and their practices of "making over" their actresses. Miles says, "You know that poor tortured soul Jimmy Stewart played in *Vertigo*? That's Hitch." Leigh says, "Compared to Orson Welles, he's a sweetheart."

When he was working on *The Birds* and *Marnie*, Hitchcock's age and privilege tricked him into playing with feelings he ordinarily kept on a very low flame, if he warmed them up at all. The evidence suggests he really did keep the flame low until these late years, so the story is not so much one of inner demons finally getting out as a story of the outer demons everyone else dealt with earlier descending on him at a time when he was ill equipped to face them.

The cruelty of Hitchcock's behavior is clear, although I take it his kindness was real enough too, and we don't have to defend him or attack him at this late date. His peculiarities, or more precisely the mixture of his genuine peculiarities with his bland, persistent ordinariness, have struck chords in millions. That is how his films work, and that is why we can't simply refer them back to a private pathology. Even if Hitchcock knew or wanted to know very little about himself, he knew a great deal about us. The question, in these late years, is how this knowledge was so largely eclipsed by his scorn for us.

Until *Family Plot,* that is.

I am probably alone in thinking that this film is almost in the same league as *North by Northwest.* If it is, this will partly be the result of the script by Ernest Lehman, who wrote both movies and who had an even more elegant novel to work with, Victor Canning's *The Rainbird Pattern.* But mainly it seems to be a matter of Hitchcock's getting his humor and his fears back by means of their old partnership.

The out-of-control car in *Family Plot* recalls a similar sequence in *North by Northwest* and not only because it is shot in a version of back projection alternating with a view of the road ahead. The whole scene is played for laughs. Our attention is held by the way the heroine is flinging her arms and legs around the hero, who is driving. The car ends up sideways, off the road, and you see the woman stiffly emerging from the top. Then there's a cut to a close-up of her espadrille supported by her partner's contorted face. He struggles out of the toppled car, and in case we're not laughing yet, his arm is seen entangled in her handbag. Yet they have been in a car careering down a mountain. The scene is not played for thrills, but the thrills are not entirely displaced by the gags.

The same sort of double take crops up in the structure of the film. Blanche Tyler (Barbara Harris) is a medium who ekes out her otherworldly talents with the help of the sleuthing she has her friend George Lumley (Bruce Dern) do for her. They are on the track of a man who is to inherit a fortune, and when they find him, they will collect a comfortable ten thousand dollars as a fee. Unfortunately, the man they are after is engaged in a series of kidnappings and thinks Blanche and George are on his trail for that.

This irony finds its perfect expression in a scene in which Blanche arrives for a conversation with a bishop who is supposed to know the whereabouts of the man she and George are after, only to witness the kidnapping of the bishop by the very same man. In the car, speeding away with their prey, the kidnappers begin to think there may be something to Blanche's psychic powers, of which they have recently, skeptically learned. After all, what else can they think? That they are in a movie governed by outrageous coincidence?

The double meaning of the title seems too obvious at first. The conspiracy and the cemetery. The family plot, like the paths of glory, leads but to the family plot. And what about the other meaning of "plot," in the sense of a story line? Is a plot in this usage still a conspiracy — against the viewer perhaps? Do all stories lead to the grave? Is that what Hitchcock meant when he wrote that every plot is the same? Is a family plot a celebration of family values, or just Freud's family romance? Let me suggest that a good narrative plot is not just a causal arrangement of events but a scheme pointing to its own scheming, a matter both of conspiracy and organization. Not every plot is a double plot, but every plot has a hint of duality about it.

What attracted him to the Canning novel, Hitchcock said, was "the structural image of those two separate plots and separate groups of characters coming gradually, inevitably together." Gradually: a question of timing. Inevitably: a question of fate. Hitchcock said that what he wanted to bring out in his treatment of the subject was in this case "something technical." Timing is certainly technical, but fate? Fate too, in the movies and many stories.

Early on in a novel, or indeed in a real-life romance, we feel that anything could happen. Then we realize what is not going to happen; different lives take different paths, settle into different shapes. We begin to feel they can't meet again. Then one day they do: The doubleness of the double plot wavers, Hitchcock's "structural image" forms. What the double plot always tells us is that there is another plot, that our plot is not the only one. What a meeting between plots tells us is that we could be in that other plot, or perhaps already are. The other plot is waiting for us, in an American cemetery say.

The cemetery is ragged, half overgrown, the pattern of the paths irregular but still a pattern. A man called Maloney has tried, on the kidnapper's instructions, to kill Blanche and George and died in the failed attempt. George thinks Maloney's widow can help him with some information and tries to talk to her after the funeral. She makes off down one cemetery path, and George takes another. The widow could avoid George if she wanted to, but that move doesn't appear to be permitted in this particular narrative game. She is not really trying to escape and George is not hurrying to meet her. It's as if they are in a labyrinth — the high-angle shot of the whole scene reinforces this effect — that has many paths but offers no escape. The paths — the widow's at the top of the screen, George's at the bottom — run parallel, turn, return to the parallel formation. The two almost meet but then continue around the sides of another, final square. *Then* they meet.

The Hitchcock scholar Lesley Brill compares the scene to the "converging rails at the beginning of *Strangers on a Train*," which is also "an emblem of plot." There are interesting differences, though. In the earlier film the lines converge and divert, forming a cross and mirroring Bruno's scheme of exchanged murders. In *Family Plot* the lines take a sudden turn and run into each other. There is nowhere else to go. The ragged cemetery suggests a world that is closed and ordered but not neat, a sort of American wilderness with a design.

In place of the wrong men, the innocents who crop up so often in Hitchcock movies here are minor frauds, faint deceivers linked to serious, genuinely murderous crooks in a chain of cupidity. But the coincidences take us back to the wrong men, because coincidence in Hitchcock is not the benign, secular deity of so many happy stories, but the meaningless instrument of extraordinary peril, the magical cause of your whole life's going wrong.

It is because Blanche sees the kidnapped bishop that the kidnapper has to try to kill her — in the novel he does kill her. She could have arrived at any other time and seen nothing. The heroes of *Frenzy, The 39 Steps,* and *North by Northwest* fall into their troubles in just the same markedly accidental way. It's not just that Blanche has found her man, come face-to-face with him, which is the most immediate narrative point. It's that Blanche has been found, by the camera and by the kidnapper, in the path of the kidnapper's plot. We have discovered through Blanche that in the world of this film you can't complete your own story without intruding dangerously on someone else's. Blanche's moaning and whimpering in her staged contact with the dead — or if you prefer, Barbara Harris's magnificent performance in this role — manages to suggest the uncanny without in any way suggesting the supernatural, and that of course is just how the coincidences work too. Hitchcock's world is governed by "ironically inappropriate injustice," as film critic Raymond

Durgnat says. Unless we wish to call it appropriate injustice, an injustice that is perfectly, horribly just in its way, since it gives us so exactly what we are afraid of, shows us what it means to be perfectly and precisely out of luck.

Old Mortality

It's good to think of this return to delicacy and eerie fun in *Family Plot,* because Hitchcock's last years did not have these elements in large quantities. He certainly insisted that *Family Plot* was not his last film, that he had another one in view. This was *The Short Night,* based on a novel by Ronald Kirkbride about George Blake, the English spy; but Hitchcock and David Freeman gave up work on it in May 1979. It did at least permit Hitchcock a grand, irreverent joke when he was knighted by the Queen of England at the end of that year. He had become, he said, "the short knight."

For a long time Hitchcock was interested in everyone's mortality except his own, as if all the dying and near dying in his works were a promise of eternal life for their orchestrator. As late as 1957 he was making jokes about what used to be his good health. A hernia operation ran into complications, but Hitchcock was undaunted — as a correspondent at least. "As one who has always boasted of never having been sick," he wrote to Michael Balcon, "I really hit the jackpot this time — Hernia, Jaundice, Gall Bladder removed — and two internal hemorrhages — all in 12 weeks." By 1964, however, his friends were dying all around him, and he felt consistently ill, without any clear diagnosis from his doctor of what was wrong. Within a few years gout was bothering him, and a pacemaker was installed in 1974. Hitchcock wrote again to Balcon to tell him the device looked like an old-fashioned fob watch.

Alma meanwhile had had a series of health scares going back to a diagnosis of cancer in 1958 and exacerbated by two strokes in 1971 and 1976. She finally lost, or was unable to sustain, her interest in a world of people and films that had always fascinated her, however much she kept her distance from it. She survived Hitchcock by two years, but by that time appears to have had no awareness that he was gone — or had been.

In 1976 Alfred and Alma took their last trip to Saint Moritz, where they had honeymooned and spent many holidays. Hitchcock had a last checkup at the Cedars-Sinai hospital and on his return home took to his bed. His doctor said that Hitchcock had years of life left in him, in spite of his various ailments and failures of function, but something in him — maybe not his will but something deeper than the will, a submerged bodily self that decides when the party is over — took control and closed the system down. Hitchcock died on April 29, 1980.

We should leave the last words to the films. It's an added pleasure that these words are not heard but only inferable from the context — a lively message from the world of silent cinema. It won't matter exactly what we imagine they are, as long as we imagine something. But we need to catch the implicit and unintended farewell. In *Family Plot* a door bears on its frosted glass the words "Registrar of Births and Deaths." Behind the glass Hitchcock, or rather a figure in the shape of his famous silhouette, is talking to a woman. He raises his finger, points it at her. His mouth moves, the woman nods, the finger points. The director is a shadow, a ghost, the moviemaker a spectral registrar. Of course Hitchcock didn't register many births in his films, but you have to be born in order to die, and he did very well in the death department. What is he telling the woman? He is saying perhaps, "You know you really shouldn't keep killing your husbands; this is the fourth time now."

Acknowledgments

Early versions of a few paragraphs in this book appeared in the *New York Review of Books* and the *London Review of Books,* and I am very grateful to the editors for allowing me to think about Hitchcock in their pages.

James Atlas knew where the book was going when I didn't, and his sharp and thoughtful suggestions helped me find the way. Elena Uribe shared every movie danger with me and saved me from countless misjudgments.

Bibliography

The books and articles on Hitchcock and his work are almost beyond number, and that's counting only the good ones. Here I list the works that I have found especially helpful, in some cases indispensable, and in which readers will find many intriguing ways of pursuing their interest in this great director.

I have relied a good deal on the excellent biographical works by Patrick McGilligan, John Russell Taylor, and Donald Spoto, and on Hitchcock's detailed conversations with François Truffaut. Most of the critical comment in this book comes from my direct and repeated contact with the films, but I would like to salute, in gratitude for their insights: Neil Badmington, Charles Barr, Claude Chabrol, Tom Cohen, Raymond Durgnat, Bill Krohn, D. A. Miller, Tania Modleski, Eric Rohmer, William Rothman, Jack Sullivan, David Thomson, George Wilson, and Robin Wood.

Auiler, Dan. *Hitchcock's Secret Notebooks: An Authorised and Illustrated Look Inside the Creative Mind of Alfred Hitchcock.* London: Bloomsbury, 1999.
———. *Vertigo: The Making of a Hitchcock Classic.* New York: St. Martin's Press, 1998.
Badmington, Neil. *Hitchcock's Magic.* Cardiff: University of Wales Press, 2011.

Barr, Charles. *Vertigo*. London: British Film Institute, 2002.

Brill, Lesley. *The Hitchcock Romance: Love and Irony in Hitchcock's Films*. Princeton, NJ: Princeton University Press, 1988.

Chandler, Charlotte. *It's Only a Movie: Alfred Hitchcock, a Personal Biography*. New York: Simon & Schuster, 2005.

Cohen, Paula Marantz. *Alfred Hitchcock: The Legacy of Victorianism*. Lexington: University Press of Kentucky, 1995.

Cohen, Tom. *Hitchcock's Cryptonymies*. Minneapolis: University of Minnesota Press, 2005.

Conrad, Peter. *The Hitchcock Murders*. London: Faber, 2000.

Durgnat, Raymond. *The Strange Case of Alfred Hitchcock*. Cambridge, MA: MIT Press, 1974.

Freedman, Jonathan, and Richard H. Millington, eds. *Hitchcock's America*. New York: Oxford University Press, 1999.

Freeman, David. *The Last Days of Alfred Hitchcock*. Woodstock, NY: Overlook Press, 1984.

Gottlieb, Sidney, ed. *Hitchcock on Hitchcock: Selected Writings and Interviews*. Berkeley: University of California Press, 1995.

Griffin, Susan M., and Alan Nadel, eds. *The Men Who Knew Too Much: Henry James and Alfred Hitchcock*. New York: Oxford University Press, 2012.

Hitchcock O'Connell, Pat, and Laurent Bouzereau. *Alma Hitchcock: The Woman behind the Man*. New York: Berkley Books, 2003.

Kapsis, Robert E. *Hitchcock: The Making of a Reputation*. Chicago: University of Chicago Press, 1992.

Krohn, Bill. *Hitchcock at Work*. London: Phaidon, 2000.

Leitch, Thomas, ed. *The Encyclopedia of Alfred Hitchcock*. New York: Facts on File, 2002.

Makkai, Katalin, ed. *Vertigo*. Abingdon, UK, and New York: Routledge, 2013.

McCarty, John, and Brian Kelleher. *Alfred Hitchcock Presents:*

An Illustrated Guide to the Ten-Year Television Career of the Master of Suspense. New York: St. Martin's Press, 1985.

McGilligan, Patrick. *Alfred Hitchcock: A Life in Darkness and Light.* New York: Regan Books, 2003.

Miller, D. A. "Hitchcock's Understyle: A Too-Close View of *Rope*," *Representations* 121, no. 1 (Winter 2013): 1–30.

Modleski, Tania. *The Women Who Knew Too Much: Hitchcock and Feminist Theory.* New York: Methuen, 1988.

Paglia, Camille. *The Birds.* London: British Film Institute, 1998.

Rebello, Stephen. *Alfred Hitchcock and the Making of* Psycho. New York: Dembner Books, 1990.

Rohmer, Eric, and Claude Chabrol. *Hitchcock, the First Forty-Four Films.* Translated by Stanley Hochman. New York: F. Ungar, 1979.

Rothman, William. *Hitchcock: The Murderous Gaze.* 1982; 2nd ed., Albany: State University of New York Press, 2012.

Spoto, Donald. *The Art of Alfred Hitchcock: Fifty Years of His Motion Pictures.* New York: Hopkinson and Blake, 1976.

——— *The Dark Side of Genius: The Life of Alfred Hitchcock.* Boston: Little, Brown, 1983.

——— *Spellbound by Beauty: Alfred Hitchcock and His Leading Ladies.* New York: Harmony Books, 2008.

Sullivan, Jack. *Hitchcock's Music.* New Haven, CT: Yale University Press, 2006.

Taylor, John Russell. *Hitch: The Life and Times of Alfred Hitchcock.* New York: Pantheon Books, 1978.

Thomson, David. *The Moment of Psycho: How Alfred Hitchcock Taught America to Love Murder.* New York: Basic Books, 2009.

Truffaut, François, with Helen G. Scott. *Hitchcock.* 1967; rev. ed., New York: Simon & Schuster, 1984.

Wilson, George M. *Narration in Light.* Baltimore, MD: Johns Hopkins University Press, 1986.

Wood, Robin. *Hitchcock's Films.* 1965; 3rd ed., South Brunswick, NJ: A. S. Barnes, 1977.

Žižek, Slavoj, ed. *Everything You Always Wanted to Know about Lacan (but Were Afraid to Ask Hitchcock).* London and New York: Verso, 1992.

Filmography

A listing of all the films in which Hitchcock had a hand, including his apprentice work and his television shows, can be found in Patrick McGilligan's biography. Here I list only the cinema films Hitchcock directed.

Number 13 (unfinished), 1922
The Pleasure Garden, 1925
The Mountain Eagle (now lost), 1926
The Lodger, 1926
Downhill, 1927
The Ring, 1927
Easy Virtue, 1927
The Farmer's Wife, 1928
Champagne, 1928
The Manxman, 1929
Blackmail (silent), 1929
Blackmail (sound), 1929
Juno and the Paycock, 1929
Elstree Calling (parts), 1930
Murder!, 1930
The Skin Game, 1931
Rich and Strange, 1931
Number Seventeen, 1932

Waltzes from Vienna, 1933
The Man Who Knew Too Much, 1934
The 39 Steps, 1935
Secret Agent, 1936
Sabotage, 1936
Young and Innocent, 1937
The Lady Vanishes, 1938
Jamaica Inn, 1939
Rebecca, 1940
Foreign Correspondent, 1940
Mr. & Mrs. Smith, 1941
Suspicion, 1941
Saboteur, 1942
Shadow of a Doubt, 1943
Lifeboat, 1944
Bon Voyage, 1944
Aventure Malgache, 1944
Spellbound, 1945
Notorious, 1946
The Paradine Case, 1947
Rope, 1948
Under Capricorn, 1949
Stage Fright, 1950
Strangers on a Train, 1951
I Confess, 1953
Dial M for Murder, 1954
Rear Window, 1954
To Catch a Thief, 1955
The Trouble with Harry, 1955
The Man Who Knew Too Much, 1956
The Wrong Man, 1956
Vertigo, 1958
North by Northwest, 1959
Psycho, 1960

The Birds, 1963
Marnie, 1964
Torn Curtain, 1966
Topaz, 1969
Frenzy, 1972
Family Plot, 1976